Tall Zarᶜa in Jordan

Report on the sondage at Tall Zarᶜa 2001-2002
(Gadara Region Project: Tall Ziraᶜa)

Jan Dijkstra
Meindert Dijkstra
Karel J. H. Vriezen

BAR International Series 1980
2009

Published in 2016 by
BAR Publishing, Oxford

BAR International Series 1980

Tall Zarʿa in Jordan

ISBN 978 1 4073 0512 7

BAR Publishing is the trading name of British Archaeological Reports (Oxford) Ltd.
British Archaeological Reports was first incorporated in 1974 to publish the BAR
Series, International and British. In 1992 Hadrian Books Ltd became part of the BAR
group. This volume was originally published by Archaeopress in conjunction with
British Archaeological Reports (Oxford) Ltd / Hadrian Books Ltd, the Series principal
publisher, in 2009. This present volume is published by BAR Publishing, 2016.

Printed in England

BAR
PUBLISHING

BAR titles are available from:

BAR Publishing
122 Banbury Rd, Oxford, OX2 7BP, UK
EMAIL   info@barpublishing.com
PHONE   +44 (0)1865 310431
FAX   +44 (0)1865 316916
www.barpublishing.com

CONTENTS

LIST OF TABLES

LIST OF GRAPHS

LIST OF FIGURES

PREFACE AND ACKNOWLEDGMENTS

On a bright day in early April 2000, a small group of archaeologists went down for a visit to the Wādī al-ᶜArab in NW Jordan. In this group were several staff members of the excavation team of the Kirchliche Hochschule Wuppertal, Germany, headed by Professor Dr Dieter Vieweger, and also two of the co-directors of the archaeological projects in Umm Qays (ancient Gadara of the Decapolis), Dr Ute Wagner-Lux and Dr Karel Vriezen. That spring, the Wuppertal team was working on a joint excavation in Baᶜja and the Umm Qays team had a study campaign processing excavation finds. The goal of the trip that day was Tall Zarᶜa, an archaeological site on an isolated hill conspicuously situated near the bottom of the wadi in the lower sector of Wādī al-ᶜArab. The tell seemed a most promising site to commence investigation of the region around the ancient city of Gadara, which was situated uphill on the plateau, *ca* 6 km to the NE and had been studied by several archaeological teams in recent decades.

After the visit, the "Region of Gadara Project" was planned and an excavation permit was applied for to the Department of Antiquities of Jordan. The permit was granted in 2001 and the project started in the same year with a large-scale survey of the site by the team of the Biblisch Archaeologisches Institut of the University in Wuppertal, headed by Dieter Vieweger, and with the excavation of a sondage, by a team of the Theological Faculty of Utrecht University in the Netherlands, headed by Karel Vriezen. The present book is the final report of the sondage, excavated in 2001 and 2002, presenting the stratigraphical and the material finds and a proposal for identification of the site.

We would like to take the opportunity to express our thanks to the Director General of the Department of Antiquities, Dr Fawwaz al-Khraysheh, and its representatives Amjad Bataineh (Irbid) and Ibrahim Zubi (Umm Qays). We also thank the Theological Faculty of Utrecht University, for making the sondage possible, and the teams of the German Protestant Institute in Amman and the Biblical Archaeological Institute in Wuppertal for their generous aid. We are indebted to Dr Gerrit van der Kooij (Tall Dayr ᶜAllā team; Leyden University), who advised us on dating the excavated pottery, to Alfred Trappenburg (Geomedia; Utrecht University), who prepared the pottery drawings for publication and to Dr K. van der Borg of the Van de Graaff laboratory, Utrecht University, for analysing the carbon-14 samples. Special thanks are due to the participants of the campaigns: Jan Dijkstra, Meindert Dijkstra, Evert van Rooijen, Gerrie van Rooijen, Erik Terwan, Peter Vreeken and Max G.L. van de Wiel from the Netherlands, and the local workmen Najib and Ahmed Muhammed Mehedad (from Kufr Asad village). Finally, we would like to thank Drs. Christopher Rigg for his generous help correcting the English text. Without all their effort, this work could not have been accomplished.

After the fieldwork and the study-campaigns in Jordan preliminary reports of the sondage have been published. Exhaustive discussions of the collected data at home helped us to work out a detailed stratigraphy and they proved once more how for a final report the old adagium applies *dies diem docet*.

CHAPTER 1

INTRODUCTION

1.1 Introduction

After three decades of archaeological work on the site of Gadara of the Decapolis, near the modern village of Umm Qays[1] in NW Jordan, the need was felt to expand the scope of research from the urban site to the surrounding region. The occupation history of ancient Gadara was brought to light in intermittent excavations by various teams since 1965. Starting as a Hellenistic fortified hill-top settlement, the city developed into one of the major urban centres in the area during Roman–Byzantine times, finally declining into a village in the Abbasid–Mamluk period.[2]

Although sherds of Iron Age pottery were also documented among the finds in the urban area, the remains of any pre-Hellenistic settlement on the site could not as yet be traced. So the question arose whether pre-Hellenistic settlements might have been elsewhere in the region. Because of the character of the archaeological remains of ancient Gadara, research had been predominantly focused on the Hellenistic–Early Islamic periods, while earlier and later periods had received only scant attention. Also the relation between the urban area of Gadara and the surrounding region had hardly yet been studied. However surveys in the areas south and west of Umm Qays had found archaeological sites with finds from various archaeological periods, including settlements, tombs and agricultural installations.[3] Especially in the area south of Umm Qays, in Wādī al-ᶜArab, many sites had been found.

So in 2001, the Gadara Region Project was started, and the tell in the centre of Wādī al-ᶜArab, Tall Zarᶜa[4] (Grid Ref. 21185/22520) was chosen as an initial focus of research. During previous visits to the site, it had been established that this tell had been inhabited almost continuously from the Early Bronze Age to the Late

Ottoman Period. The project commenced with a large-scale survey of the tell by a team of the Biblical Archaeological Institute (BAI) of the University in Wuppertal (Germany), headed by Dieter Vieweger, 10 September–9 October 2001.[5] A team of the Theological Faculty of the University in Utrecht (Netherlands), headed by Karel Vriezen, continued the project by excavating a sondage or test trench[6] in order to probe the stratigraphy in two campaigns, 21 October–1 November 2001 and 19–31 October 2002,[7] which were followed by three study-sessions in 2004, 2005 and 2006. From 2003 on, the team from the BAI Wuppertal conducted campaigns every year, in cooperation with the German Protestant Institute of Archaeology in Amman, headed by Jutta Häser from 2004.[8]

1.2 The Site

Tall Zarᶜa is situated in the western sector of Wādī al-ᶜArab, which runs from the Transjordanian highlands near the city of Irbid to the Jordan Valley near northern Shūnah (Fig. 1.4). The site is a conspicuous tell, situated on the south side of the wadi, east of the confluence with the Wādī ez-Zahar near the storage lake, that developed after the Wādī al-ᶜArab dam was completed in the 1980s (Fig. 1.1). The top plateau of the tell is almost circular, ca 160 m in diameter and rises for ca 20 m over the surrounding fields to the south and more than twice that height to the north, where the fields slope down to the wadi. In the centre of the plateau, is a pool with reeds and canes growing. Its artesian well supplies fresh water. Geo-electrical measurements, which were part of the large-scale survey by the Wuppertal team in 2001, established that the tell consisted of a natural hill covered with an accumulation of archaeological layers 6–12 m thick on top.[9]

1.3 Previous Investigations

The importance of the tell had already been recognized by G. Schumacher,[10] who visited the site and described the remains of rectangular buildings with walls composed of limestone and basalt ashlars in his notes.[11] He also mentioned an ancient traffic route going up from northern Shūnah in the Jordan Valley through Wādī al-ᶜArab to

---

[1] For the representation of Arabic place-names in Jordan the system of transliteration of the *Annual of the Department of Antiquities of Jordan* is used.
[2] For a summary of the archaeological results, see Weber 2002.
[3] Schumacher, 1890: 108–110, 142–143; Steuernagel, 1926:70–83; Glueck, 1951: 182–184; Mittmann, 1970: 24–39, 133–138, 169–179; Kerestes *et al.*, 1978: 129; Hanbury-Tenison, 1984: 385–423; Weber and Hübner, 1998: 453–455; Riedl, 1999: 45–48.
[4] In this report, the name of the site is transcribed according to the style of the *Annual of the Department of Antiquities of Jordan*. Other transcriptions are JADIS 1994 (Tell Zerᶜah); Kerestes *et al.* 1977/78 (Tell Zerᶜah); Reicke and Rost 1979 (Tell Zerᶜa); Glueck 1951 (Tell Zerᶜah); Schumacher 1890 (Tell Zara'a), Clauß 1907 (tell Zara'a); Steuernagel 1926 (tell zaraᶜa); Hanbury-Tenison 1984 (Tell Ziraᶜa) and Vieweger and Häser (Tell Zerāᶜa / Tell Ziraᶜa).

[5] Vieweger, 2002a, 2002b.
[6] The term sondage has been used throughout this report.
[7] Vriezen, 2002a, 2002b, 2003; Dijkstra *et al.* 2005a; Dijkstra *et al.* 2005b.
[8] Vieweger and Häser, 2005, 2007a, 2007b.
[9] Vieweger, 2005: 8–9; Vieweger and Häser, 2007b: 149.
[10] Schumacher, 1890, 110,142-143.
[11] Published by Steuernagel, 1926: 81.

Bayt Rās / ancient Capitolias and then splitting to aṭ-Ṭurra and the Golan, and to Darʿā and Syria. He also mentioned remains of ancient strongholds and Ottoman watermills.[12] In his *Karte des Ostjordanlandes*, the tell is marked as inhabited.[13]

Half a century later, in 1942, N. Glueck visited the site and described the ancient remains as follows:

> "The uneven, terraced top of the hill of Tell Zerʿah was at one time completely enclosed within a strong fortification wall, some parts of which are still visible, particularly on the n. side. This wall probably hails back to the Early Bronze period. Numerous foundation remains are visible on top of the hill, belonging to buildings erected from Roman through mediaeval Arabic times…In addition to the water of the spring, we saw two large cisterns on top of the *tell*, and there may be others, which like them may have been dug in Roman or Byzantine times."[14]

In his surface finds, pottery from Early Bronze I–III, Iron Age I–II, the Roman, Byzantine and Mediaeval Arabic periods are listed. Then, in preparation of the construction of the reservoir dam, the tell was surveyed by two archaeological teams.

In 1978 the team of T.M. Kerestes, J.M. Lundquist, B.G. Wood and K. Yassine surveyed it, mentioning

> "… abundant foundations and building stones. One large cistern …. a floor of tesserae about .5 m below the surface. The sherds collected were predominantly from the Late Byzantine period, with also a good representation from the Early Bronze period."[15]

And in 1983, a team headed by J.W. Hanbury-Tenison thoroughly surveyed three areas in the western, the central and the eastern sectors of the wadi, documenting over a hundred sites, mentioning for Tall Zarʿa "occupation of all periods, Chalco/EB to mediaeval. Cisterns, casemate walls (?), and mediaeval structures". Two members of this team later published a study of the Ottoman watermills in the Wādī al-ʿArab.[16]

Encouraged by this data from the archaeological literature and by private visits to the tell in 2000, it was decided to apply for a permit to excavate on Tall Zarʿa as a key-site for a long-term archaeological project of the Region of Gadara.

FIG. 1.1 STORAGE LAKE IN WĀDĪ AL-ʿARAB. VIEW FROM TALL ZARʿA

FIG. 1.2 TALL ZARʿA VIEW FROM E

FIG. 1.3 TALL ZARʿA VIEW FROM S (UMM QAYS IS LOCATED UPHILL)

---

[12] Steuernagel, 1925: 93–94, cf. Schumacher, 1890: 109–111.
[13] Steuernagel, 1926: 81.
[14] Glueck, 1951: 184.
[15] Kerestes *et al.*, 1978: 129.
[16] Gardiner and McQuitty, 1987; McQuitty, 1995.

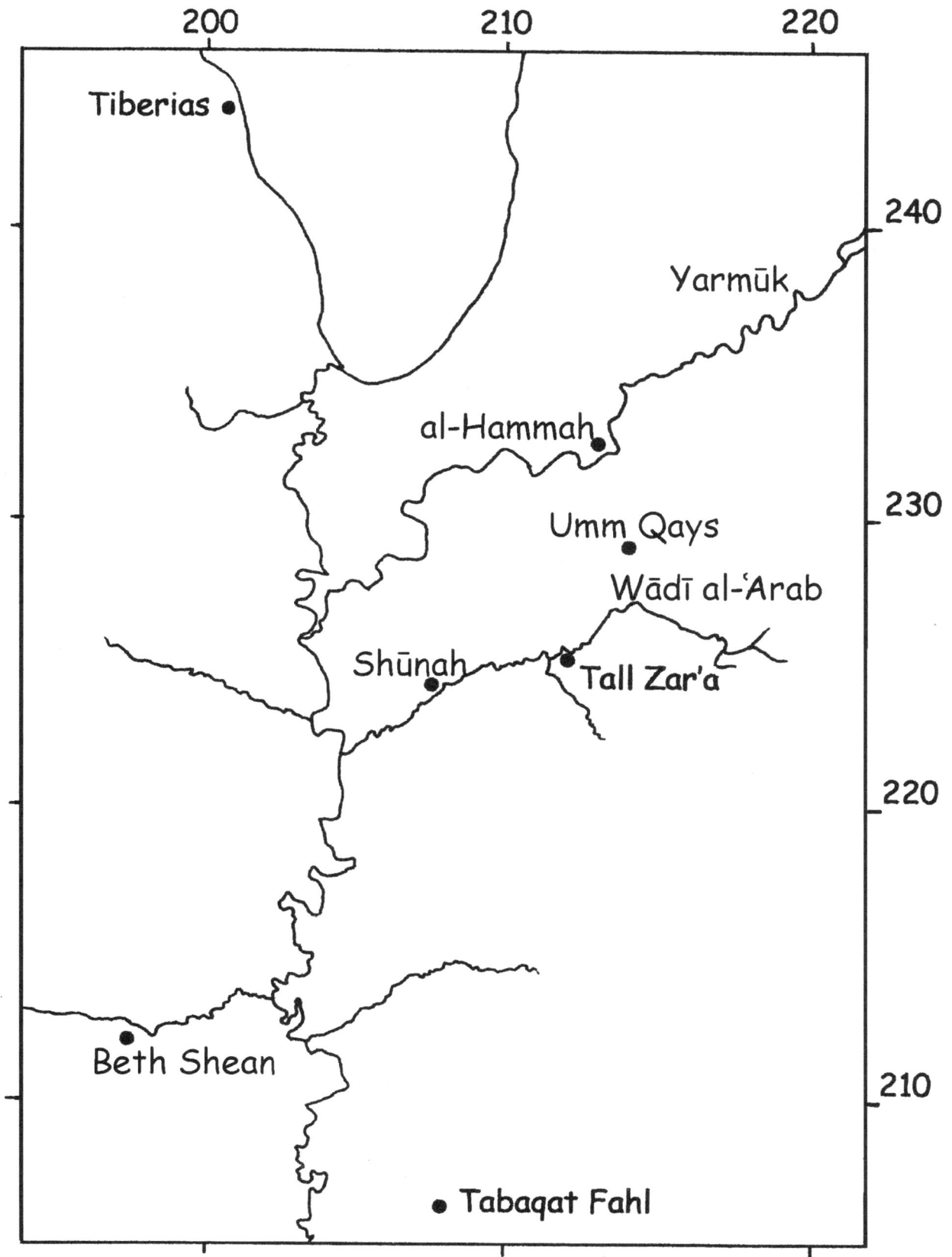

Fig. 1.4 Map of Tall Zarᶜa and surrounding area.

2.1 The Trench

The trench, measuring 6 m × 6 m, was excavated on the western edge of the tell plateau (Fig. 2.4), coordinates of the NE corner of the trench are 2117783-2252144. Before the dig three parallel walls were visible on the surface, encircling the western part of the plateau. It was supposed that they might be the remains of an ancient defence line and therefore the sondage was laid out as to cross these walls. In 2001, a trench measuring 4,50 m × 6,00 m was opened and was enlarged to a 6,00 m × 6,00 m trench during the 2002 campaign (Fig. 2.5).[1] Occasionally, building remains in the area immediately west of the trench were exposed, enlarging the exposure to 7,00 m × 6,00 m (Fig. 2.7;2.19). The situation of this western extension on the surface of the slope with recent intrusions, however, made it unsuitable for the stratigraphical analysis that had been intended. While removing the Early Islamic Stratum I, a line of walls (Walls W4, W5 and part of W1) running E–W, the total length of the trench on the S side was discovered and left unexcavated (including part of Wall W1), limiting the area of the trench to *ca* 5,00 m × 6,00 m for the lower strata.

The surface layer (20 cm.) yielded a great variety of ceramic finds dating from the Mamluk, Omayyad and Roman–Byzantine periods, as well as the Iron Age. Below, the following five strata were discovered.

2.2 Stratum I. Islamic Period

Phase I.1
The youngest phase was a pit (Pit P1; 2,00 m × 1,20 m; depth 1,00 m), in which Late Islamic (Mamluk) ceramics were found (Fig. 2.1;2.6).

Phase I.2
The youngest building phase was the N–S Wall 1 (W1 in diagrams) and the accompanying cobblestone Floor Fl.A, which had been laid to the east, and, where it had been lost, there was a greyish earthen layer (Fig. 2.1;2.16–2.19). Wall W1 (0,90–1,00 m wide) had been constructed of hewn limestone blocks with smaller fieldstones in between and functioned as a retaining wall for a courtyard or a street, surfaced mainly with cobble stones, on the south side, however, with flagstones. Wall W1 had

been built on an older N–S wall of the Late Roman/Early Byzantine period (Phase II.1, Wall W7). In our preliminary report,[2] we suggested Wall W1 to be a terrace wall situated together with the cobble-stone floor outside an ancient settlement. This interpretation was amended after the more extensive excavations by the teams of the University of Wuppertal and the German Protestant Institute, exposing more Early Islamic building remains nearby.[3]

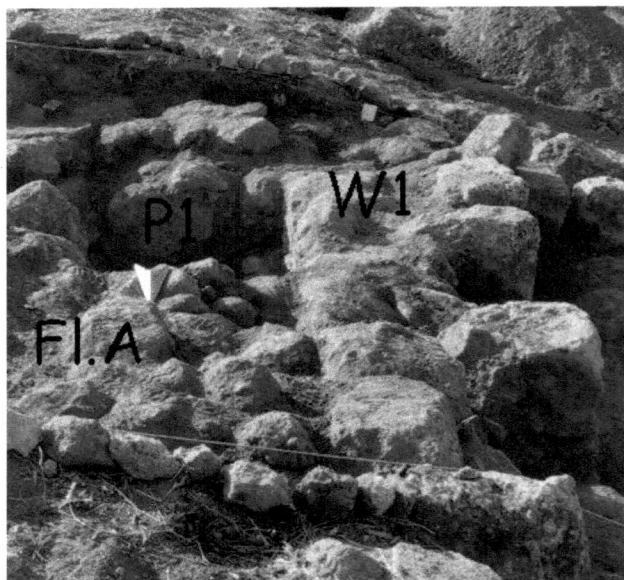

FIG. 2.1 PHASES I.1 - I.2 (PIT P1; FLOOR FL.A; WALL W1)

Phase I.3
In the eastern part of the sondage, Wall W6 ran N–S, while Walls W3 and W4 are E–W. Between them was an accumulated deposit 0,20–0,30 m thick of four earthen floors with some cobblestones (together Floor Fl.B). Each of these floors was 0,02–0,10 m thick: lead-coloured with ash, white mortar, light-brown and lead-coloured (Floor Fl.B in Fig. 2.2;2.7;2.17-19;2.22-23). Wall W6 (1,10 m wide) had been constructed of hewn limestone blocks in the two lower courses and field stones in the courses above. Wall W3 (0,70–0,80 m wide) was visible only in the E section (Fig. 2.18) and, possibly, there was a doorway between it and Wall W6. Wall W4 (1,00 m wide) had been constructed of limestone blocks and joined with Wall W6.

---

[1] The stratigraphical units excavated are numbered in two series: the 1.-series for the layers in the 2001-trench and the 2.-series for the enlargement area of 2002. The contents of the stratigraphical units are numbered according to the layer nos. (the find nos.). Here, the layers and their finds will be indicated TZ+serial no. (e.g. TZ 1.1).

[2] Dijkstra et al. 2005b, 177–178.
[3] Vieweger and Häser, 2007a, 21–22.

Phase I.4

In the western part of the sondage, the N–S Wall W2 was discovered (Fig. 2.7;2.16-17;2.19;2.24). This wall is 0,80–0,90 m wide and had been constructed of hewn limestone blocks and boulders on a foundation of field stones. Because of the later construction of Wall W1 and of the building stones fallen between Walls W2 and W1, any traces of floors accompanying Wall W2 were lost, and so we could not establish whether there was any relationship between Walls W2 and W6.

Also Wall W5 (Fig. 2.7;2.19) was regarded as part of Phase I.4, as this wall, just like Wall W2, had been built upon a *tannūr* belonging to Stratum II, Phase 1 (see below). The constructions of Phases I.3 and I.4 (Floor Fl.B, Walls W6, W3, W2, W4 and W5) seemed to belong together as one building phase.

West of the sondage trench remains of a N–S wall were visible from the onset, its relation to the finds in our sondage were uncertain, as recent intrusions had blurred the stratigraphy here. (Wall Wz in Fig. 2:7;2.19).

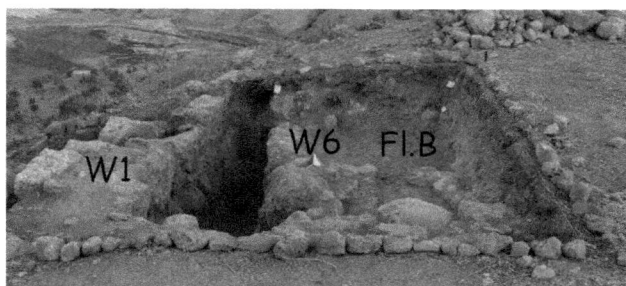

FIG. 2.2: PHASE I.3 (WALL W6; FLOOR FL.B; WALL W1)

2.3 Stratum II. Late Roman/Early Byzantine Period

Phase II.1

Under the deposit of yellow earth, in which Wall W2 was set, was a 0,10–0,20 m thick loamy Floor Fl.C. On this floor were the remains of several bread ovens. Two ovens were still *in situ*. They were of the free-standing *tannūr* type[4] with a cylindrical to slightly tapering wall. The southern one of these *tanānīr* (Fig. 2.3;2.8: O1; diam. 0,76 m at the base, still standing to 0,36 m) was set on a circle of fieldstones and had a double-faced wall of an outer and an inner wall (each 3,5–4,0 cm thick) and a hollow space (2,0 cm wide) in between, which in antiquity may have been filled with soft material.[5] Inside Oven O1 there was a complete, although smashed, cooking pot, which had apparently been placed in the oven while still hot after baking bread.[6] The northern one (Fig. 2.3;2.8;2.24-25: O2) had a diam. of 0,48 m at the base, still standing up to 0,15 m and had a wall thickness

of 4,0 cm. On Floor Fl.C, various other ovens may have once stood as the numerous *tannūr* fragments witness. One of these ovens (Fig. 2.8: O3) was built to the SE of Oven O1, wall to wall, and had been built over by Wall W5, which may indicate that Wall W5 was contemporaneous to Wall W2 and may belong to Phase I.4. Floor Fl.C ran east to the N–S Wall W7 (1,02 m wide). This Wall W7 appeared almost to follow the same course as the later N–S Wall W1 (Phase I.2), its eastern part lying underneath Wall W1 (Fig. 2.8; 2.16-2.17; 2.19). By the finds in Floor Fl.C and in Wall W7 and by the cooking pot inside Oven O1, Phase II.1 may be dated as Late Roman-Early Byzantine (2nd–4th Century CE) (Fig. 4.2:1).

FIG. 2.3 PHASE II.1 (OVENS O1-O2; COOKING POT TZ 1.22; WALL W5)

Phase II.2.

Underneath Phase II.1, there was another loamy floor, Floor Fl.D, in part separated from Floor Fl.C by a 0,20 m thick earthen layer, in part directly under Floor Fl.C. Floor Fl.D was related to the E–W Wall W8, which ran eastwards underneath Wall W7 and westwards against the N–S Wall W9 (Fig. 2.9;2.26-27).[7] Parallel to each other in Floor Fl.D were three shallow gullies or channels 0,10 m wide, sunk down to the underlying red soil. Their use may have been related to the *tanānīr* that were situated on Floor D, as the many *tannūr* fragments on this floor witness.[8]

2.4 Stratum III. Iron Age IIB

The remains of the Early Islamic period (Phase I.2–3) and of the Late Roman/Early Byzantine period (Phase II.1–2) were laid down on layers dating from the Iron Age II. These were generally reddish. Occasionally, it was difficult to discern a clear interface between those higher strata and Stratum III, as the soil was apparently mixed in the level of contact by digging and intrusions from the younger strata. The layers with mixed contents have all been classified to the younger Strata I–II: TZ 1.8; 1.9;

---

[4] Dalman, 1935, 91–93; McQuitty, 1993, 56f.; Fritz and Kempinski, 1983, 110.
[5] Dalman, 1935, 102; Abb. 18:6; McQuitty, 1993, 63-65; Briend and Humbert, 1980, 31-32; cf. Fritz and Kempinski, 1983, 112; Chambon, 1984, 37-38; Steen, 1991, 139.
[6] See for a similar find: Steen, 1991, 153, Pl. I.2.

[7] Wall W9 is more or less in the same absolute level as Wall Wz and probably next to it, but as the latter is outside the sondage, it could not be established whether there is any relation between the two.
[8] These gullies may have been part of the ventilation system. Dalman, 1935, 89; Steen, 1991, 141.

1.10; 2.30. The layers, in which walls and floors from Strata I-II were found, were also excavated together with earth below: TZ 1.12; 1.25; 1.26; 2.19; 2.25; 2.28; 2.30; 2.35. For description of the excavated layers, see Table 2.1.

Phase III.1

In the reddish earth deposit, on which Walls W6 and W1, and accompanying layers were situated, there were few remains of floors and layers of ash. This deposit lay on a layer of mortar 4 cm thick, Mortar M1, in the NE part of the sondage (Fig. 2.18). It extended as a thin loamy layer southwards. Among other finds, the deposit contained some nearly complete ceramic vessels (Fig. 4.3:13). In the NE quarter of the sondage, Mortar M1 covered a cobble-stone floor, Floor Fl.E, on which a complete Iron Age chalice was found (Fig. 4.3:7). It is not clear whether Mortar M1 was itself a floor covering Floor Fl.E or whether it was the remains of washed-down walls of houses associated with Floor Fl.E. In the SE corner, a heap of field stones was uncovered (Fig. 2.18-19).

Phase III.2

In the NE quarter of the sondage, the cobble-stone Floor Fl.E, was associated with Walls W11 and W12 and lay on other floors related to these walls, Floors Fl.F and Fl.G, each 2–4 cm thick (Fig. 2.10;2.16-18;2.28-30). Wall W11 ran E–W and Wall W12 ran N–S. Both were made of boulders and field stones and were 0,50–0,60 m thick. The scanty remains of a floor and of the supposed Wall W10, visible in the S section, were possibly associated with these successive Floors Fl.F–Fl.G and Walls W11 and W12 (Fig. 2.10;2.19), together constituting the remains of an Iron Age II house in the eastern part of the sondage. The remains of a broken millstone incorporated into Wall W7 may also once have belonged to the contents of this house.

Phase III.3

Underneath Floors Fl.F–Fl.G of Phase III.2, there was a deposit of reddish earth accumulated on a layer of ash. This deposit was 0,20 m thick near the east section and gradually thickened westwards to 0,34 m near Wall W12.

2.5 Stratum IV. Iron Age IA/B–IIA

Phase IV.1

A layer of ash (4–6 cm thick) covered the eastern half of the sondage. It runs up to Walls W13, W14 and W17 further west. However the remains of the ash layer were not recovered all over the area. This may be seen in the N, S and E sections, in which it also was visible how the layer tended to slope westwards being 0,40–0,50 m lower in the central part of the sondage than near the E section (Fig. 2.17–19). There was also a slope for the floors and layers below, perhaps because of the large pit, which was once situated at a lower level in the central part of the sondage (Phase IV.5) and which may have caused layers of Phases IV.1–4 to give way under the heavy load of later walls, such as Walls W12, W13, W7 and W1. On the S side under Wall W7, the ash layer had filled a depression 0,38 m deep (Fig. 2.19, S section). The

ash layer covered a yellowish deposit of earth, also sloping and decreasing from 0,20 m thick in the E section to 0,06 m at 1,70 m to the west.

Phase IV.2

Underneath this deposit was a light grey floor 3 cm thick, Floor Fl.H, while between Walls W14 and W17, the ash layer was deposited directly on Floor Fl.H (Fig. 2.17–2.19). In this floor were three shallow pits with charcoal ca 5 cm deep; diam. 0,75 m near N section; diam. 0,55 m near E section; diam. 0,40 m near the SE corner of the sondage (Fig. 2.11), in which there were the remains of Early Iron Age cooking pots (Fig. 4.7:9). Floor Fl.H was associated with Walls W13, W14, W15, W16 and W17, but could not be traced in the whole area. It was visible from the NE corner of the sondage for ca 2 m to the W and for ca 2,5 m to the E, between Walls 14 and 17, and in the SE corner for 0,5 m to the N and for 1,5 m to the W and possibly down in the depression under Wall W7. In the walls, there were two openings, one between Walls W13 and W14 near the N section, and one between Walls W15 and W16 near the E section.

On Floor Fl.H, various complete or nearly complete pots were discovered (Fig. 4.6:5,6; 4.7:9,11), perhaps this area was abandoned with the pots left standing on the floor. Thereafter a layer of yellowish earth accumulated and a layer of ash (Phase IV.1) was deposited. One of the complete pots discovered was a Iron Age I cooking pot on the shallow fire-pit (Fig. 2.11; 4.7:9; Find no. TZ 2.33). The charcoal from this pit was taken to the R.J. van de Graaff laboratory in Utrecht for analysis, which gave a 14C Age 2983 ± 50 [BP] and a Calender age 3077–3243 [cal BP].[9]

During the processing of the ceramic finds, some sherds from this phase proved to be related to sherds from the fill of the large pit, which had been in this area before (Phase IV.5).[10] So the layers of this phase had tipped and slid a little, as the fill of the earlier large pit subsided. Probably for this reason, Floor Fl.H was not found to be a continuous layer in the area S of Walls W15–W16.

Phase IV.3

Below Floor Fl.H was a layer of reddish soil ca 0,15 m thick deposited on a grey Floor Fl.I (2 cm thick). This floor ran as far as the same walls as in Phase IV.2. On the N side, it ran as far as Wall W14, and may once have continued to Wall W17. In the central area of the sondage, it linked to Walls W13 and W16 (Fig. 2.12;2.31). But Wall W15 did not then exist. In the E section was visible how Floor Fl.I sank down southwards to gain its original level again near the S section (Fig. 2.17–19). In the floor of the room between Walls 16 and 13, there was a stone circle around a shallow pit filled with ash (diam. 1,20 m).

---

[9] UtC No. 15085.
[10] Connections of sherds from Find nos. TZ 1.38+1.42, TZ 1.39+1.50 and TZ 2.44+1.50. Compare also Table 2.1, Stratigraphical units with contents.

Circa 0,1 m lower was another light-grey Floor Fl.J (2 cm thick) in which there were three shallow pits with ash, diam. 0.20–0.35 m (Fig. 2.13;2.32-33). West of Wall W13, field stones and boulders were removed by us from what may have been a western continuation of Wall W16.[11] In the E section was visible that Floor Fl.I lay directly on Floor J and that together they sloped to the S, because of a large pit of Phase IV.5 in the SE quarter of the sondage, whose fill had compacted and given way. During the processing of the ceramic finds, some sherds from this phase could be connected to sherds from the fill of the large pit of Phase IV.5.[12]

Phase IV.4
Under Walls W13 and W16 and Floor Fl.J was another Floor Fl.K (2 cm thick) on which were a large millstone and five shallow pits with ash (diam. 0,30–0,40 m; Fig. 2.14;2.17;2.33-34). Floor Fl.K sealed a large pit of Phase IV.5.

Phase IV.5
The large pit mentioned above extended in the south and central part of the sondage area. As the character of the fill in the SE quarter of the sondage differed a little from that of the central-western part, we labelled these Pit 2 and Pit 3, respectively (Fig. 2.14-15, P2 and P3). During the processing of the ceramic finds, however, there were two matches of connecting sherds from the fills of Pit 2 and Pit 3.[13] This is an indication of contact between the two fills. They were probably, contemporaneous. The same may also be true for these Pits P2 and P3.

Pit P2 in the SE quarter of the sondage was filled with layers of refuse that had slid in from the S and it contained remains of many broken mud-bricks and ash mixed with grey-brown soil, and with a layer of yellowish loamy soil that had slid in from the N (Fig. 2.14-15; 2.18-19, E and S sections: hatched). The sondage probably did not reach the bottom of this fill or its southern end. In the north, this fill may have accumulated against the S side of Wall W20 (Phase V.1). It is unclear whether Floor Fl.K extended S of the 225212 line, as no traces were found to confirm this. Any remains of such a southern extension may have disappeared into the subsiding fill of Pit P2. The fill perhaps consisted of an upper and a lower part, which then should be numbered Pit P2a and Pit P2b.[14] The fill of Pit P2a, above -21,70 m, originated from a brick wall built on a stone foundation visible in the S section and tentatively labelled Wall W18 (Fig. 2.14;2.19;2.35). A floor related to this supposed wall might have been in the same horizon as Floor Fl.K. This phase was dated by a charcoal sample, analysed at the R.J. Van de Graaff

laboratory, to 14C Age 2920 ± 50 [BP], Calender age 2991–3160 [cal.BP];[15] the pottery was mixed and assigned to Late Bronze – Iron Age IIA.[16] The lower part of the fill (below –21,70 m) postulated in this way, P2b, may then have come from a lower brick building (Phase V.2), the pottery finds here also were mixed dating from Middle Bronze IIC – Iron Age I.[17]

Pit P3 extends E–W in the central-western part of the sondage and was filled with reddish earth with some field stones and boulders. This part of the large pit had been dug into a thick deposit of yellowish loamy soil still extant at the N side and in the SW quarter of the sondage (Fig. 2.14-15;2.33-34) and well contrasting with the reddish fill. Pit P3 was *ca* 1,00 m deep in the centre of the sondage, shallower near its northern edge. Under Floor Fl.K in Pit P3 were some large fragments of Iron Age I pottery as well as Middle Bronze IIC–Late Bronze I pottery.[18] In the pit was an E–W line of accumulated boulders, which may be the remains of a lower wall running through the centre of the sondage, Wall W20 (Phase V.1). The pit, here, cut through a mud-brick N–S Wall W19 (Phase V.2).

Although this phase is presented as the last layer in Stratum IV, the observation that parts of the Floors Fl.H-Fl.K slid into Pits P2 and P3 and mixed with their fill, implies that in the fill finds contemporaneous with those of the floors occur.

2.6 Stratum V. Late Bronze Age–Iron Age IA

Phase V.1
The E–W line of field stones and boulders exposed in the lower part of Pit P3 seemed to continue to the E, where the tops of stones became visible at the level where the sondage stopped under Floor Fl.K. It may be supposed that this line of stones and its continuation formed an E–W Wall W20 (Fig. 2.15). In the E half of the sondage the soil to the N of the supposed Wall W20 was yellowish and hard loamy, while to the S it was reddish and greyish like the fill of Pits P3 and P2. In the W half, Pit P3 was on both sides of Wall W20, but, on the N side the pit was shallower than on the S side. As Wall W20 cuts through the older N–S Wall W19, which we suppose to be dated to the Late Bronze (Phase V.2), we suggest that Wall 20 was built in the Iron Age IA.

Phase V.2
Pit P3 seemed to have cut through the N–S mud-brick wall, Walls W19–W19a in the W half of the sondage area, as was visible in the S section (Fig. 2:19;2.35). The wall was made up of two brick walls. The western one, Wall W19, is 1,00 m wide and still stood 0,90 m high, six layers of bricks (65/78 × 36/42 × 8/12 cm) upon two (or perhaps more) layers of field stones. The mud-bricks of the eastern Wall W19a lay on a layer of gravel and had

---

[11] In removing these stones, Find nos. TZ 2.43, TZ 2.47 and TZ 2.49 were probably contaminated with finds from the surface layer.
[12] Connections of sherds from Find nos. TZ 1.50+2.49+2.54; TZ 1.50+2.54; TZ 1.61+2.54; TZ 1.44+1.49 and TZ 2.39+2.43+2.44+ 2.45+2.50+2.51. Cf. also Table 2.1, Stratigraphical units with contents.
[13] Connections of sherds from Find nos. TZ 1.50+2.49+2.56 and TZ 1.61+1.62. Compare also Table 2.1, Stratigraphical units with contents.
[14] However the match of four sherds from both Pit 2a and Pit 2b (from Find nos. TZ 1.47+1.49+1.59+1.61) does not favour this suggestion.

[15] UtC No. 15084.
[16] Fig. 4.3: 6,9,12; 4.4: 1,2; 4.5: 2,4,8; 4.7: 3; 4. 8: 2,10,14,16,24,27.
[17] Fig. 4.5: 1,7,10,12,14; 4.6: 8; 4.7: 4,8; 4.8: 4,5,7,17,23,26.
[18] Fig. 4.4: 20,21; 4.8: 28.

deteriorated, only three layers of bricks had survived with a total width of 0,40 m, the tipping lines of the fill of Pit P2b starting right from their edge. The wide space 1,40 m between Walls W19 and W19a was solidly packed with yellowish loamy soil. It is unclear whether this was a casemate between two mudbrick walls later filled up with loamy soil, or whether this was meant to be a solid core sandwiched between two mud-brick faces. A deposit of yellowish loamy soil had washed from the top of Wall W19 to the west.

The NE part of the sondage was stopped at a depth of -21,35 m, the NW part at -21,82 m, on a higher level than the S half, which stopped at -22,60 m. In the W part of the N section (Fig. 2.17) a tumble of several layers of mud-bricks from Wall W19 was visible in the yellowish loamy soil deposit. In the E part of the N section too, a tumble of mud-bricks was seen in the same deposit. However without further information, it was uncertain whether they also originated from a wall in this area. The yellowish loamy deposit, in which Pit P3 had been sunk, was visible west of Wall W19 in the S section (Fig. 2.19) and in the lower part of the N section (Fig. 2:17). In our opinion, it was the decay of unbaked mud bricks of ancient buildings. The individual orange-brown bricks discerned in this deposit were baked. We hardly delved into this loamy deposit but stopped near the interface between this and the deposits above. The considerable number of Bronze Age ceramic sherds mixed in with the finds in Pits P2 and P3 suggested that this loamy deposit, together with Walls W19–W19a, were of the Late Bronze Age.

2.7 Tables of finds

In Tables 2.1–2.3, the Find nos.[19] and stratigraphic phases, and their contents are described according to the observations and counts in the field. Byz., Byzantine Period; E, East; EIsl, Early Islamic Period; He, Hellenistic Period; IA, Iron Age; LB, Late Bronze Age; LIsl, Late Islamic Period; MB, Middle Bronze Age; N, north; Rom., Roman Period; S, south; Undia., Undiagnostic and as such not assigned ; W, west.

---

[19] Here, the indication Find no. (=Layer no.) is used for stratigraphical units (cf. Footnote 1).

Table 2.1 Stratigraphical units with contents (H, homogeneous; F, few; M, many). [20]

TZfindno /Phaseno.	Description	MB-LB	IA	He	Rom.	Byz	EIsl	LIsl	Un-dia.	Other
1.B	surface layer		15		33		54	19	199	1 mill-stone
1.1/I.1	contents of Pit P1		18		20		29	25	69	
1.2/I.2	grey earth layer		20		18		67		35	
1.3/I.2	fallen building stones		67	4	163	11	147	4	249	
1.4/I.2	fallen building stones		11		16		54	6	103	
1.5/I.2	cobble-stone Floor Fl.A									
1.6/I.2	yellow earth under TZ 1.5		14		14		41		60	F bones
1.7/I.3	Floor Fl.B, cobble-stones, yellow earth		122		13		30		45	2 glass, M bones
1.8/I.3	red earth under TZ 1.1		8		3	3	13		26	
1.9/I.3	red earth under TZ 1.7		95		2				3	M bones
1.10/I.3	brown earth under TZ 1.1/1.8		42		80		31	1	139	F bones, 1 glass
1.11/I.4	yellow earth E/W of Wall W2 (cf. TZ 2.20)		70		23		34		121	M tannursh F bones
1.12/I.3	Wall W6+red-brown earth below		72		2				25	F bones
1.15/I.4	Wall W2 + earth below		5		4		1		52	F tannur sherds. 1 glass
1.17/I.2	Wall W1		26	3	25		25	2	172	
2.B	surface layer		8		36	3			117	1 sling-stone
2.18	surface layer		5		23				75	H tannur sherds F bones.
2.2/I.2	with TZ 2.5, grey earth		8		12	2			35	1 sling-stone
2.3/I.2	fallen stones (cf. TZ 1.3)		5		17				133	F bones
2.4/I.4	yellow earth under TZ 2.3		30		26				193	1 sling-stone, F bones
2.5/I.2	cobblestone Floor Fl.A									
2.6/I.3	yellow earth E of Wall W6 (cf. TZ 1.7)		16		1		1		17	1 mill-stone F bones
2.7/I.3	yellow earth, W of Wall W6 (cf. TZ 1.8, TZ 2.6)		7		11				56	4 sling-stones
2.8/I.4	Wall W2+earth W of Wall W2	1	14	1	5				32	F bones
2.9/I.2	Wall W1		6		12	10			46	F tannur sherds. 1 mill-stone
2.10/I.3	Wall W6		4		2				8	1 mill-stone
2.13/I.4	yellow earth W of Wall W2		6		6				37	
2.16/I.2	Wall W1		7		19				7	F bones
2.20/I.4	yellow earth under Wall W2 (cf. TZ 1.11)		8		6	18			42	F tannur sherds.
1.13/II.1	Floor Fl.C (and intrusion?) (cf. TZ 2.17)		46		14		10		100	
1.18/II.1	tannur built in lower Wall W1				2				5	
1.19/II.1	In or around Oven O2		9		2		4		3	M tannur sherds.
1.20/II.1	In / around Oven O1		39		18		13		74	F bones M tannur sherds.

[20] The values homogeneous (H), few (F) or many (M) are for bones: F is <10, H is 10–20, M is >20, and for *tannūr* sherds F <5, H 5–10, M >10. These values are calculated as follows. The total number of bones found is 1228 occurring in 74 Find nos., which makes the average occurrence 16. The total number of *tannūr* sherds is 234, occurring in 34 Find nos., which makes the average occurrence 7. The classes F, H, M are deduced from the average occurrence.

TZfindno /Phaseno.	Description	MB-LB	IA	He	Rom.	Byz.	EIsl	LIsl	Un-dia.	Other
1.22/II.1	Cooking pot in Oven O1				55					Cooking pot.
1.23/II.1	red earth under Floor Fl.C		57							
1.24/II.2	dark beige earth under TZ 1.13/1.23	4	141	1	3		2		71	F bones
1.25/II.2	grey brown earth under TZ 1.24	12	162	1	6		1		33	M bones
1.26/II.1	Wall W7	6	119		19		10		40	F tannur sherds. F bones spindle wheel.
1.41/II.1	Wall W7	1	30		2		2		13	F bones
2.17/II.1	Floor Fl.C (cf. TZ 1.13)		3		3	1			47	F bones, ash, H tannur sherds.
2.19/II.1	red earth directly E of Wall W7 (cf. TZ 1.26)	1	26		3	1			4	H bones; 1 chalice
2.21/II.2	grey earth under TZ 2.20 (cf. TZ 1.24)	1								F bones F tannur sherds. 1 glass
2.24/II.1	Floor Fl.C + grey earth below		42	1	12	3			80	F bones, F tannursh. 1 glass 1 sling stone
2.25/II.2	part of Floor Fl.D + red earth below (cf. TZ 2.28)		4						3	charcoal, F tannur sherds.
2.27/II.1	cleaning Wall W7		5		1	2			4	
2.28/II.2	part of Floor Fl.D (cf. TZ 2.25)	6	69	1	2	3	1		49	F bones, M tannur sherds. 2 sling stones
2.29/II.1	lower stones of Wall W7	2	12		11	14			44	F tannur sherds. 1 mill-stone
2.30/II.1	Red-brown earth under Wall W7, west of Wall W12	10	108		2	5			58	F bones, ash F tannur sherds, 1 mill-stone, 1 flint
2.35/II.2	Wall W8 + two boulders below (down to thick Iron Age[?] layer of ash from TZ IV.1 (cf. TZ 1.33; TZ 2.44)	1	26		2	2			12	
1.14/III.1	locus: of Iron Age jar		23							F bones
1.16/III.1	Red-brown earth under TZ 1.12, TZ 1.14, TZ 1.10		62						18	M bones, F tannur sherds.
1.21/III.1	Red-brown earth under TZ 1.9, TZ 1.16		138						44	M bones
1.27/III.1	Red-brown earth deposit on Mortar M1	2	37						3	H bones
1.28/III.1	dark red-grey earth deposit on Wall W10	1	81							M bones
1.29/III.1	Red-brown earth under mill-stone in Wall W7		5							F bones, Mill-stone
1.30/III.1	Red-brown earth deposit S of Wall W11	2	39							F bones

TZfindno /Phaseno.	Description	MB-LB	IA	He	Rom.	Byz	EIsl	LIsl	Un-dia.	Other
1.31/III.1	Mortar M1 N of Wall W11	1	39						4	F bones, F tannur-sherds.
1.32/III.2	Floors Fl.F and Fl.G		31							F bones
1.35/III.3	Red-brown earth with grits and gravel, N of Wall W11, deposit on layer of ash		21						2	F bones
2.11/III.1	red earth below Wall W6 towards E		40		1				3	F bones
2.12/III.1	red earth below Wall W6 towards W		24		2				37	M bones
2.14/III.1	red earth below Wall W6		16						2	F bones
2.15/III.1	red earth E of Wall W1	6	101						77	F bones, 1 mill-stone, 2 flints
2.22/III.1	Chalice on Floor Fl.E		61						2	M tannursh., Chalice
2.23/III.2	Floor Fl.E N of Wall W11	2	128		2	2			7	F bones, charcoal, F tannur sherds, flints, 2 sling-stones
2.26/III.3	Red-brown earth with grits and gravel, below TZ 2.23, deposit on layer of ash (cf. TZ 1.35;TZ 2.35)	3	106		1	1			36	H bones, 1 mill-stone
2.36/III.2	Floors Fl.F and Fl.G	6	77		1				2	1 flint
1.33/IV.1	dark grey-brown with gravel, layer of ash and Floor Fl.H									
1.34/IV.2	locus in Floor Fl.H of hearth (cf. TZ 2.32, TZ 2.33)									
1.36/IV.1	Layer of ash									
1.37/IV.2	Floor Fl.H	5	168							M bones
1.38/IV.2	Iron Age pot on Fl.H	1	47						9	
1.39/IV.2	Iron Age pot on Fl.H		97							
1.40/IV.1	Layer of ash									
1.42/IV.3	under Floor Fl.H and layer of ash	10	327							M bones, F tannur sherds.
1.43/IV.5	Fill of Pit P2a: ash, rubble, mud bricks	13	25						271	M bones, 1 sling-stone
1.44/IV.5	Fill of Pit P2a	4	60						3	M bones
1.45/IV.3	Floors Fl.H and Fl.I	2	37						9	
1.46/IV.5	Fill of Pit P2a: ash, rubble, mud bricks	7	73							H bones 3 sling-stones, 1 mill-stone, 1 flint, 1wea-ving weight
1.47/IV.5	hearth in fill of Pit P2a	2	12							F bones
1.48/IV.5	Fill of Pit P2b, yellowish soil washed down, Wall W18 in SW quarter	12	117							M bones 3 mill-stones

TZfindno /Phaseno.	Description	MB-LB	IA	He	Rom.	Byz	EIsl	LIsl	Un-dia.	Other
1.49/IV.5	Fill of Pit P2a: broken mud-bricks and ash	33	629		1					M bones, M charcoal, 2 flints, 1 weaving weight, 1 spindle wheel.
1.50/IV.5	Fill of Pit P2a: waste washed down from Wall P18 (ash, light grey and orange, bricks)	21	241						3	M bones, F tannur sherds, charcoal, 3 flints
1.52/IV.5	Pit P2b, brown earth in yellowish loamy fill	1								F tannur sherds.
1.53/IV.5	Pit P2b, brown earth in yellowish loamy fill		1						7	
1.54/IV.5	Fire pit (?) in fill of Pit P2b	4	64						8	F bones, F tannur sherds., 1 spindle wheel
1.59/IV.5	Pit P2b, fill with mortar and pestle	9	290							M bones, H tannur sherds., 1 sling-stone, 1 basalt bowl
1.61/IV.5	Fill of Pit P2b	23	34							M bones, F tannur sherds., 1 spindle wheel.
2.31/IV.1	yellow earth deposit on Floor Fl.H (cf. TZ 2.44)	16	274						17	M bones, F tannur sherds., 1 sling stone
2.32/IV.2	Hearth in N of Floor Fl.H		4							M ash
2.33/IV.2	Hearth in E of Floor Fl.H (cf. TZ 1.34)		16							M ash, F tannur sherds.
2.34/IV.3	Reddish earth on Floor Fl.I and stone circle (diam. 1,20 m) with ash	3	35							H bones 1 flint
2.37/IV.3	Wall 16 under Floor Fl.H	8	124							M bones, 2 flints, 1 piece of copper ore
2.38/IV.1	On floor with tannur west of TZ 2.25	9	111		1	1				F bones, F tannur sherds.
2.39/IV.3	Earth between Floors Fl.H and Fl.I	11	136		2					M bones, F tannur sherds, M charcoal
2.40/IV.3	Hearth in Floor Fl.J		3							M charcoal
2.41/IV.3	Hearth in Floor Fl.J		11		2					H bones F charcoal
2.42/IV.3	Hearth in Floor Fl.J									
2.43/0.0-IV.3	Stones in W continuation of Wall W16?		15	2					4	F bones

TZfindno /Phaseno.	Description	MB-LB	IA	He	Rom.	Byz	EIsl	LIsl	Un-dia.	Other
2.44/IV.1	Red earth between Walls W14 and W13 on Floor Fl.H.	2	27							F bones ash, 1 sling-stone
2.45/IV.3	Stones in W continuation of Wall W16?		2							1 mill-stone
2.46/IV.2	Red-brown earth under Wall W8 down to Wall W14	1	15							F bones
2.47/0.0-IV.3	under TZ 2.38, mixed with surface finds	3	4	2						
2.49/0.0-IV.3	under TZ 2.47 on accumulation of stone mixed with surface finds	6	104	3	3	4			1	M bones 1 flint 3 mill-stones
2.50/IV.5	Pit P3, locus of Iron Age[?] pots in fill under Floor Fl.K	1	84							H bones M tannur sherds.
2.51/IV.5	Pit P3, locus of Iron Age pot in fill under TZ 2.50	3	147						1	F bones, F tannur sherds., 1 spindle wheel.
2.52/IV.3	Floor Fl.J	10	166			1				H bones, 1 weaving weight.
2.53/IV.3	Under TZ 2.44 on Floor Fl.J	1	4							
2.54/IV.3	Wall W13	7	40							F bones 1 basalt rolling pin
2.55/IV.3	Wall W16	5	37							F bones 1 flint
2.56/IV.4	Floor Fl.K and down to stone deposit below (S half)	33	527			1				M bones H tannur sherds. 2 sling-stone s, 1 mill-stone
2.57/IV.4	Floor Fl.K and down to yellowish soil below (N half)	7	118							M bones F tannursh. 2 flints 1 slingstone
2.58/IV.5	Pit P3, fill below TZ 2.50–51		609							M bones, H tannursh., 2 slingstone 1 millstone
1.51/V.2	Yellowish loamy soil under TZ 1.48	9	9							1 spindlewh. F bones F tannursh.
1.55/V.2	Quick lime in Wall W19a		19						4	F bones
1.56/V.2	Wall W19, core and yellowish loamy soil									
1.57/V.2	Yellow brick									
1.58/V.2	Dark red-brown brick	3	3	1						
1.60/V.2	Wall W19, core and W of it yellowish loamy soil, with bricks	2	59							H bones F tannur sherds. 1 mill-stone

TZfindno /Phaseno.	Description	MB-LB	IA	He	Rom.	Byz	EIsl	LIsl	Un-dia.	Other
1.62/V.2	Solid yellowish loamy soil	7	136							H bones F tannur sherds. 1 sling-stone 1 mill-stone
2.38.1/V.2	Yellowish loamy soil; arrow-head (cf. TZ 2.48)		4							bronze arrow-head
2.48/V.2	Yellowish loamy soil (cf. TZ 2.38.1)	1	39							
2.59/V.2	Yellowish soil under Pit.V.1)	3	37							F bones 1 flint 1 sling-stone

Table 2.2 Totals of ceramic finds in Table 2.1.

TZ Find no. /Phase no.	MB-LB	IA	Hel	Rom.	Byz.	E.Isl.	L.Isl.	Un-dia.	Totals
Totals	366	7777	17	767	78	575	57	3310	12947

Table 2.3 Stratigraphical units with ceramic contents arranged according to stratum and phase. Abbreviations and codes as in Table 2.1. Differences in value are indicated by brackets. [21]

TZ Find no. /Phase no.	MB-LB	IA	Hel	Rom.	Byz.	E.Isl.	L.Isl.	Un-dia.	Totals
1.B		(15)		33		54	19	199	320
2.B		(8)		36		3		117	164
2.18		(5)		23				75	103
Totals Surface		(28)		92		57	19	391	587
1.1/I.1		(18)		20		(29)	25	69	161
Totals I.1		(18)		20		(29)	25	69	161
1.2/I.2		(20)		18		67		35	140
1.3/I.2		(67)	4	163	11	147	4	249	645
1.4/I.2		(11)		16		54	6	103	190
1.5/I.2									
1.6/I.2		(14)		14		41		60	129
1.17/I.2		(26)	3	25		25	2	172	253
2.2/I.2		(8)		12		2		35	57

[21] There is much diversity in the values of the data noted in Table 2.3. Some phases have only very modest totals of sherds, while in other phases individual epochs may be represented only very poorly. In order better to balance the data and to eliminate intrusive sherds, the table was "cleaned" by establishing minimal values as follows. As a minimal value of the total number of sherds per phase, the next-lower decade under 10 % of the average number per phase was taken: total of sherds found 12 947, total of phases with sherds 16, average per phase 809, 10 % of 809 is 81, so 80 is minimal value per phase, if the number of sherds ≤80 the content of the phase is 0.

As a minimal value for the finds of individual epochs, we took the average value of these finds per phase divided by two. The total of MB / LB sherds is 366, they were found in 13 phases, which makes an average of 28 sherds. So, if the value of MB / LB sherds ≤ 14, then the value equals 0. The minimum value for IA sherds is 243, for Hell. sherds 2, for Roman sherds 32, for Byz. sherds 4, for Early Isl. sherds 48, for Late Isl. sherds 7, for the Undiagnostic sherds 110.

TZ Find no. /Phase no.	MB-LB	IA	Hel	Rom.	Byz.	E.Isl.	L.Isl.	Un-dia.	Totals
2.3/I.2		(5)		17				133	155
2.5/I.2									
2.9/I.2		(6)		12	10			46	74
2.16/I.2		(7)		19				7	33
Totals I.2		(164)	7	296	21	336	12	840	1676
1.7/I.3		122		13		30		45	210
1.8/I.3		8		3	3	13		26	53
1.9/I.3		95		2				3	100
1.10/I.3		42		80		31	(1)	139	293
1.11/I.4		70		23		34		121	248
1.12/I.3		72		2				25	99
1.15/I.4		5		4		1		52	62
2.4/I.4		30		26				193	249
2.6/I.3		16		1		1		17	35
2.7/I.3		7		11				56	74
2.8/I.4	(1)	14	1	5				32	53
2.10/I.3		4		2				8	14
2.13/I.4		6		6				37	49
2.20/I.4		8		6	12			42	68
Totals I.3+I.4	(1)	499	1	184	15	110	(1)	796	1607
1.13/II.1		46		14		(10)		100	170
1.18/II.1				2				5	7
1.19/II.1		9		2		(4)		3	18
1.20/II.1		39		18		(13)		74	144
1.22/II.1				55					55
1.23/II.1		57							57
1.26/II.1	6	119		19		(10)		40	194
1.41/II.1	1	30		2		(2)		13	48
2.17/II.1		3		3	1			47	54
2.19/II.1	1	26		3	1			4	35
2.24/II.1		42	(1)	12	3			80	138
2.27/II.1		5		1	2			4	12
2.29/II.1	2	12		11	14			44	83
2.30/II.1	10	108		2	5			58	183
Totals II.1	20	496	(1)	144	26	(39)		472	1198
1.24/II.2	4	141	1	(3)		(2)		71	222
1.25/II.2	12	162	1	(6)		(1)		33	215
2.21/II.2	1								1
2.25/II.2		4						3	7
2.28/II.2	6	69	1	(2)	3	(1)		49	131
2.35/II.2	1	26		(2)	2			12	43
Totals II.2	24	402	3	(13)	5	(4)		168	619
1.14/III.1		23							23
1.16/III.1		62						18	80
1.21/III.1		138						44	182
1.27/III.1	(2)	37						3	42
1.28/III.1	(1)	81							82

TZ Find no. /Phase no.	MB-LB	IA	Hel	Rom.	Byz.	E.Isl.	L.Isl.	Un-dia.	Totals
1.29/III.1		5							5
1.30/III.1	(2)	39							41
1.31/III.1	(1)	39						4	44
2.11/III.1		40			(1)			3	44
2.12/III.1		24		(2)				37	63
2.14/III.1		16						2	18
2.15/III.1	(6)	101						77	184
2.22/III.1		61						2	63
Totals III.1	(12)	666		(2)	(1)			190	871
1.32/III.2		(31)							31
2.23/III.2	(2)	(128)		(2)	(2)			(7)	141
2.36/III.2	(6)	(77)		(1)				(2)	86
Totals III.2	(8)	(236)		(3)	(2)			(9)	258
1.35/III.3		(21)						(2)	23
2.26/III.3	(3)	(106)		(1)	(1)			(36)	147
Totals III.3	(3)	(127)		(1)	(1)			(38)	170
1.33/IV.1									
1.36/IV.1									
1.40/IV.1									
2.31/IV.1	16	274						(17)	307
2.38/IV.1	9	111		(1)	(1)				122
2.44/IV.1	2	27							29
Totals IV.1	27	412		(1)	(1)			(17)	458
1.34/IV.2									
1.37/IV.2	(5)	168							173
1.38/IV.2	(1)	47						(9)	57
1.39/IV.2		97							97
2.32/IV.2		4							4
2.33/IV.2		16							16
2.46/IV.2	(1)	15							16
Totals IV.2	(7)	347						(9)	363
1.42/IV.3	10	327							337
1.45/IV.3	2	37						(9)	48
2.34/IV.3	3	35							38
2.37/IV.3	8	124							132
2.39/IV.3	11	136		(2)					149
2.40/IV.3		3							3
2.41/IV.3		11		(2)					13
2.42/IV.3									
2.43/0.0-IV.3		15	2					(4)	21
2.45/IV.3		2							2
2.47/0.0-IV.3	3	4		(2)					9
2.49/0.0-IV.3	6	104	3	(3)	4			(1)	121
2.52/IV.3	10	166			1				177
2.53/IV.3	1	4							5
2.54/IV.3	7	40							47
2.55/IV.3	5	37							42

TZ Find no. /Phase no.	MB-LB	IA	Hel	Rom.	Byz.	E.Isl.	L.Isl.	Un-dia.	Totals
Totals IV.3	66	1045	5	(9)	5			(14)	1144
2.56/IV.4	33	527			(1)				561
2.57/IV.4	7	118							125
Totals IV.4	40	645			(1)				686
1.43/IV.5 (P2a)	13	25						271	309
1.44/IV.5 (P2a)	4	60						3	67
1.46/IV.5 (P2a)	7	73							80
1.47/IV.5 (P2a)	2	12							14
1.48/IV.5 (P2a)	12	117							129
1.49/IV.5 (P2a)	33	629		(1)					663
1.50/IV.5 (P2a)	21	241						3	265
Totals IV.5 P2a	92	1157		(1)				277	1527
1.52/IV.5 (P2b)	1								1
1.53/IV.5 (P2b)		1						(7)	8
1.54/IV.5 (P2b)	4	64						(8)	76
1.59/IV.5 (P2b)	9	290							299
1.61/IV.5 (P2b)	23	34							57
Totals IV.5 P2b	37	389						(15)	441
2.50/IV.5 (P3)	1	84							85
2.51/IV.5 (P3)	3	147						(1)	151
2.58/IV.5 (P3)		609							609
Totals IV.5 P3	4	840						(1)	845
1.51/V.2	9	9							18
1.55/V.2		19						(4)	23
1.56/V.2									
1.57/V.2									
1.58/V.2	3	3		(1)					7
1.60/V.2	2	59							61
1.62/V.2	7	136							143
2.38.1/V.2		4							4
2.48/V.2	1	39							40
2.59/V.2	3	37							40
Totals V.2	25	306		(1)				(4)	336

After the exercise of "cleaning" (Footnote 20), Table 2.3 shows which ceramic finds may be seen as intrusive sherds. These are set between brackets. Only the totals of Phase IV.3 are beyond what stratigraphically may be expected: they show numbers of more recent sherds (Roman and Byzantine) exceeding the minimum qualifying them as intrusive. This anomaly may be accounted for by limited mixture with surface soil in layers TZ2.43, TZ2.47 and TZ2.49.

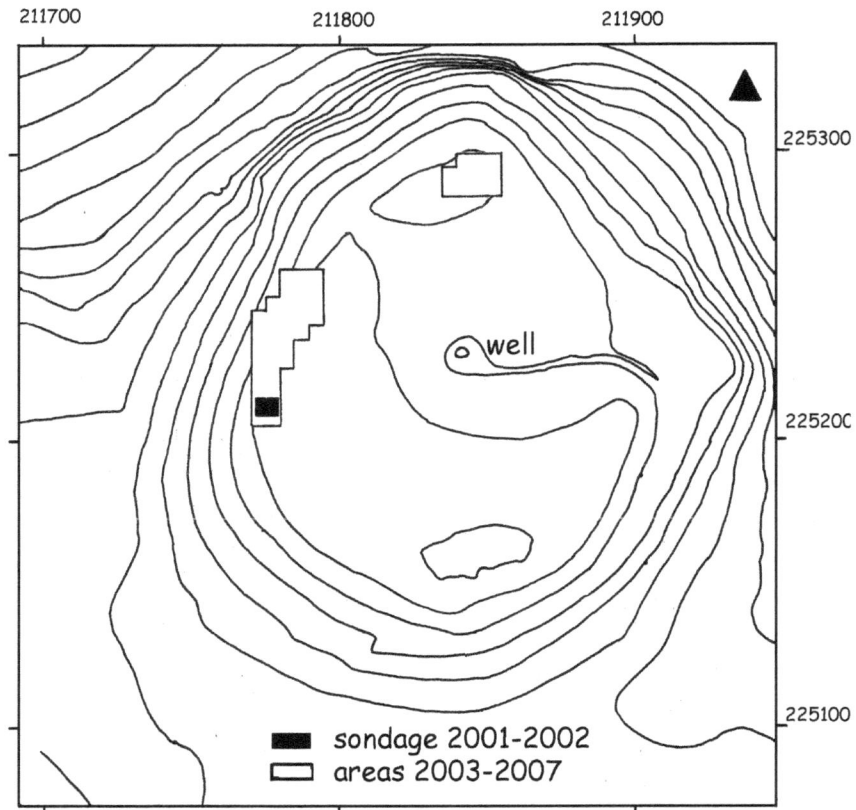

FIG. 2.4 PLAN OF TALL ZAR^{C}A: SONDAGE AND EXCAVATION AREAS.

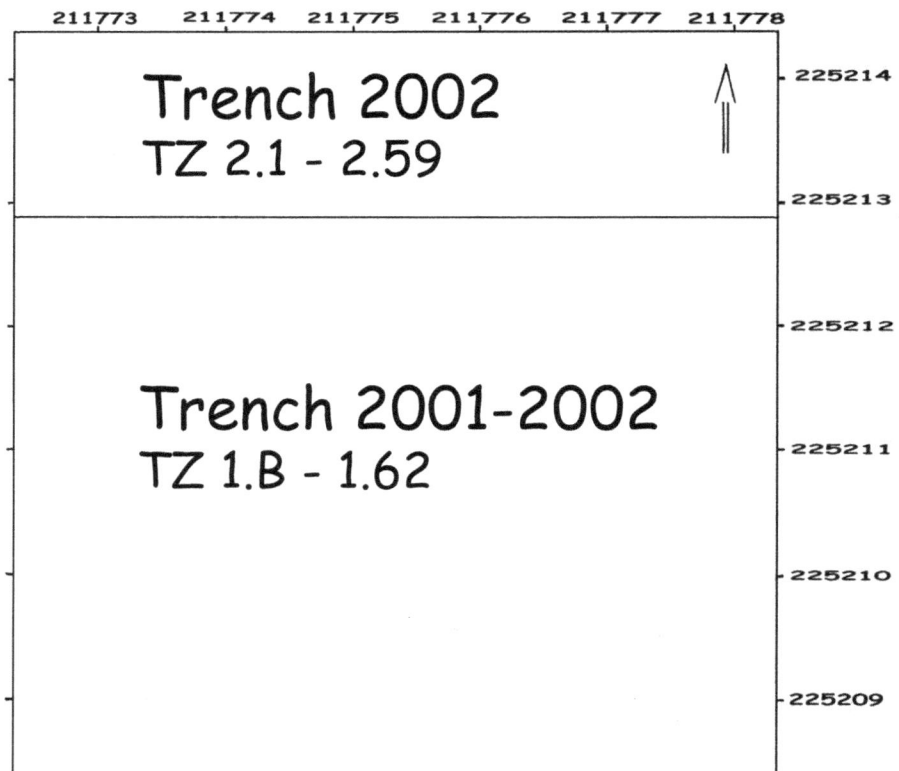

FIG. 2.5 TALL ZAR^{C}A: PLAN OF SONDAGE, TRENCH 2001–2002.

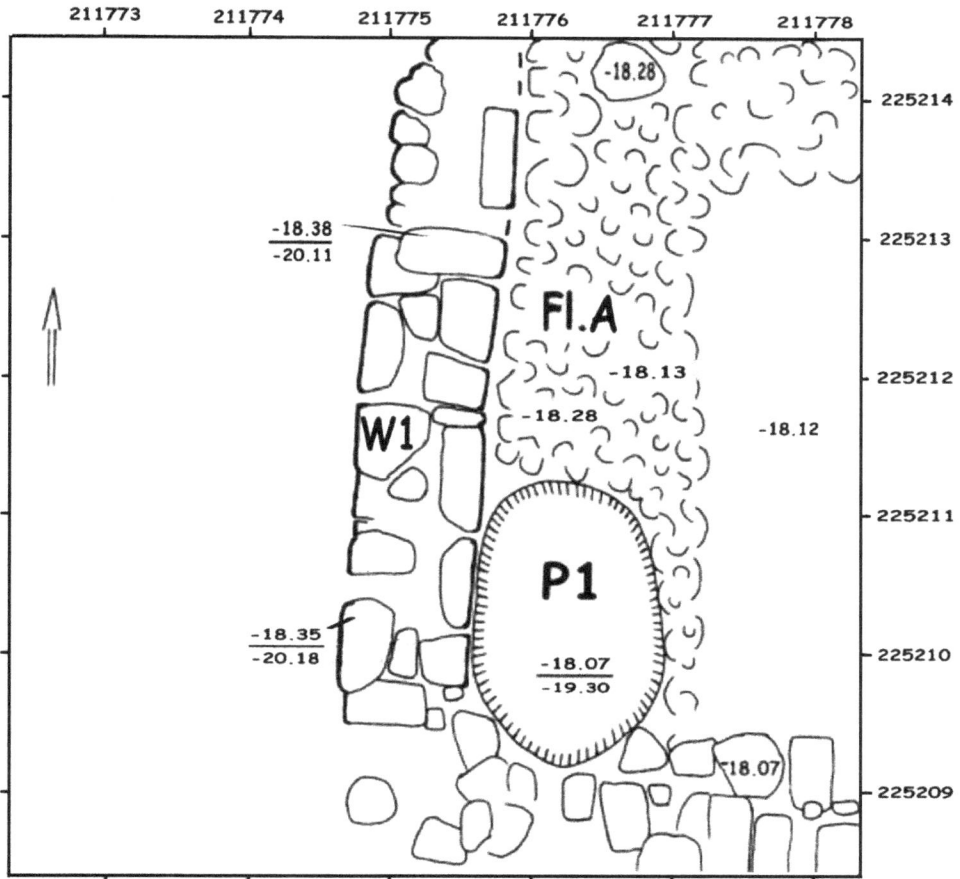

FIG. 2.6 TALL ZAR^cA: PLAN OF SONDAGE PHASES I.1–I.2.

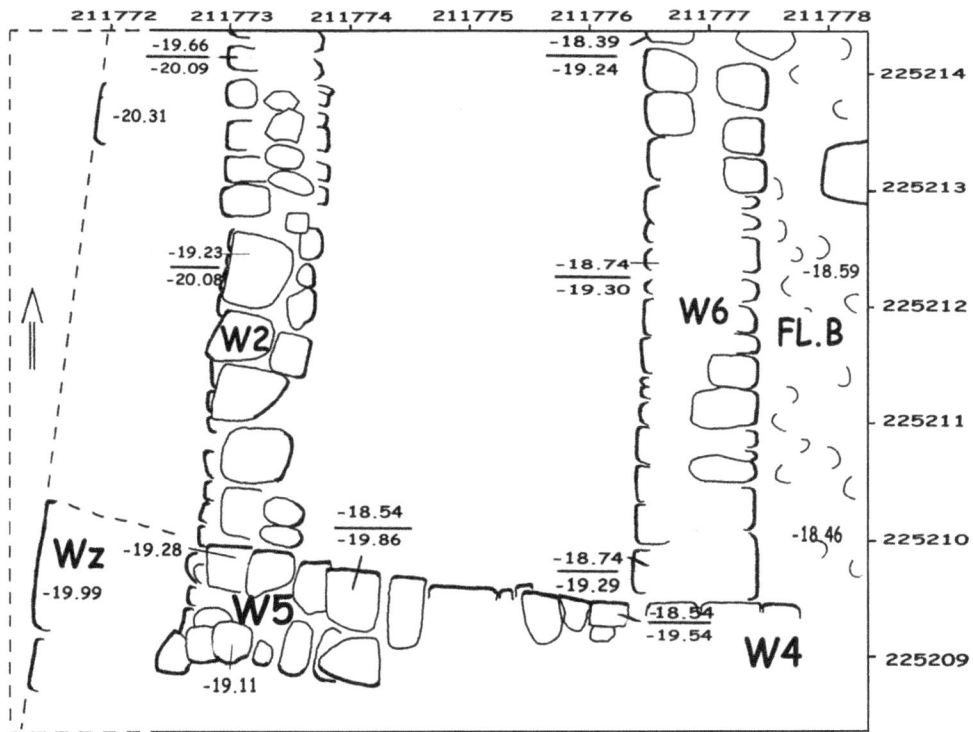

FIG. 2.7 TALL ZAR^cA: PLAN OF SONDAGE PHASES I.3–I.4.

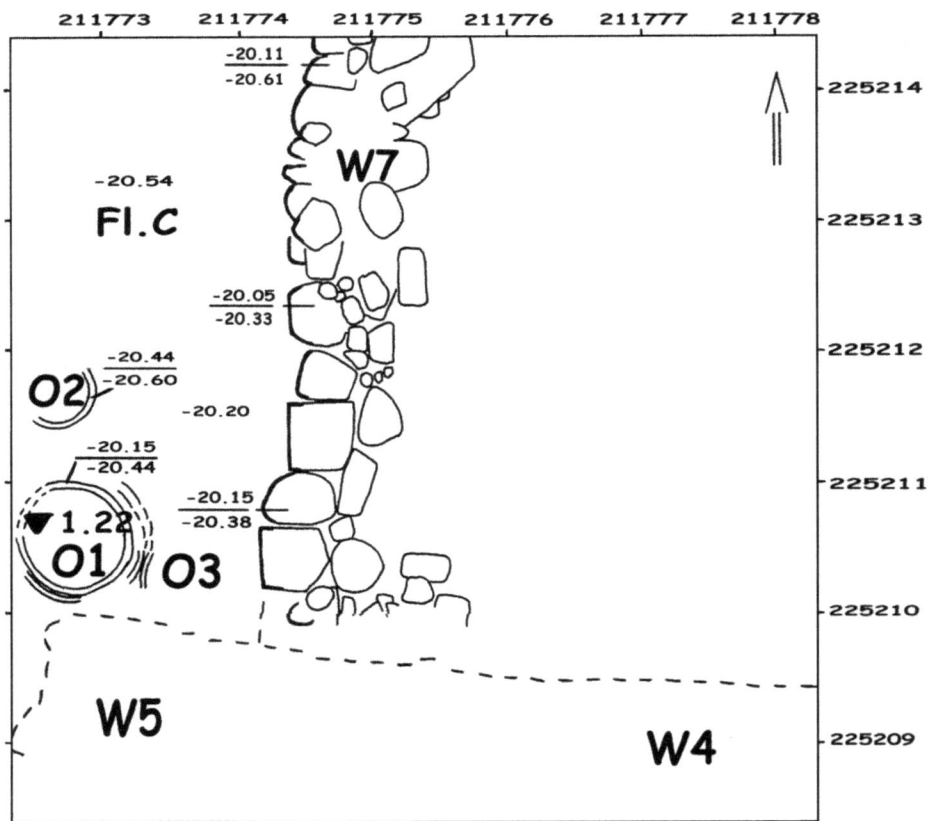

FIG. 2.8 TALL ZAR^{C}A: PLAN OF SONDAGE PHASE II.1.

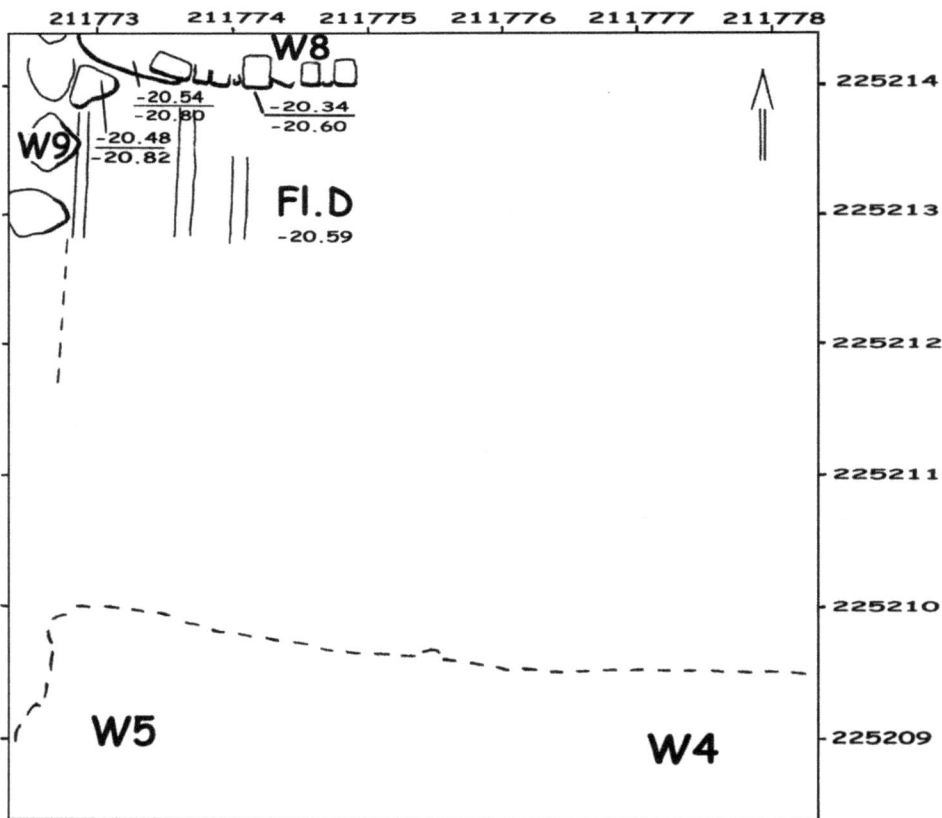

FIG. 2.9 TALL ZAR^{C}A: PLAN OF SONDAGE PHASE II.2.

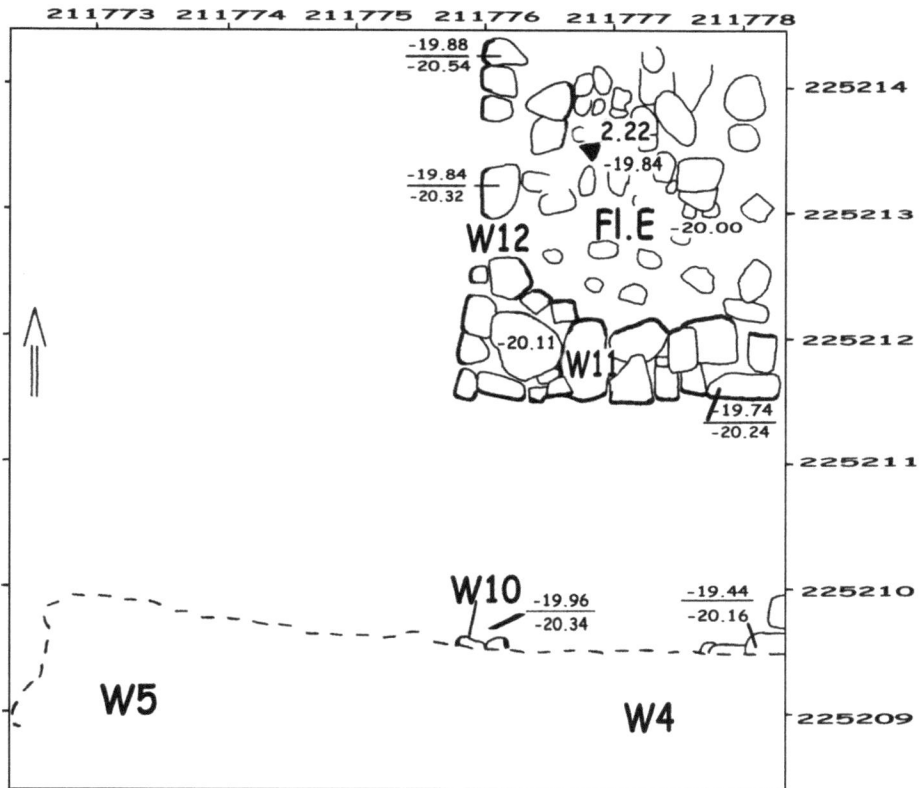

FIG. 2.10 TALL ZAR^{C}A: PLAN OF SONDAGE PHASE III.2.

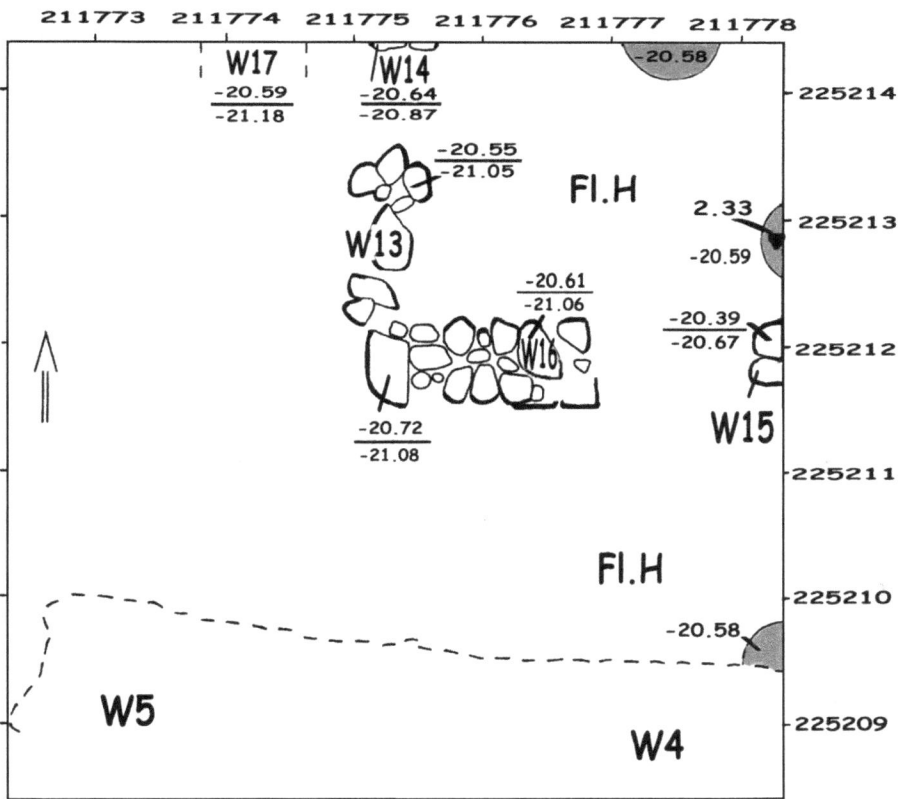

FIG. 2.11 TALL ZAR^{C}A: PLAN OF SONDAGE PHASE IV.2.

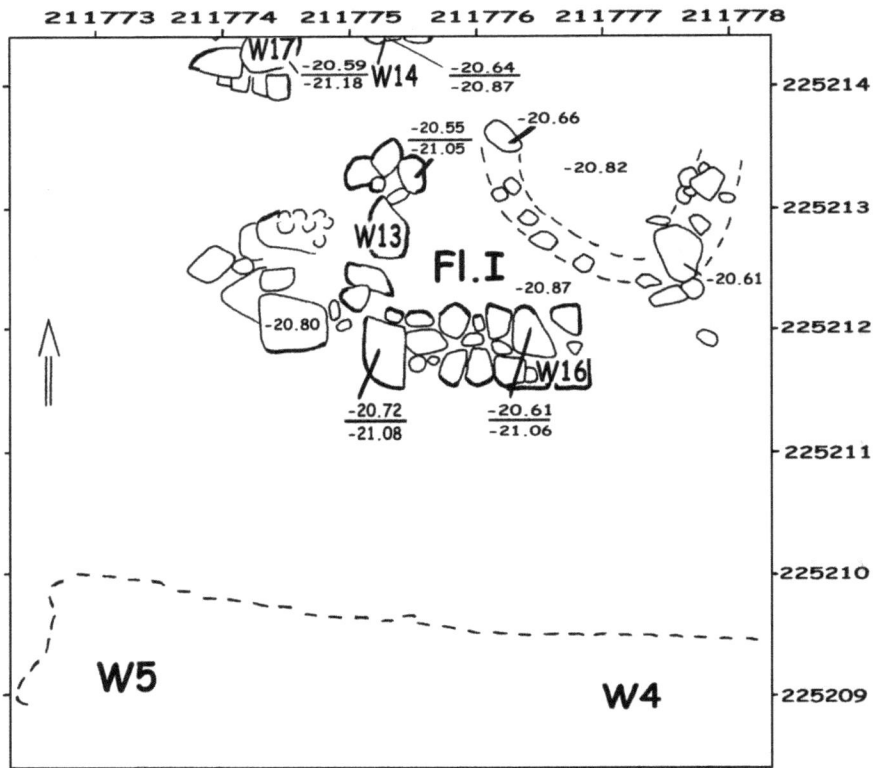

FIG. 2.12 TALL ZAR^{C}A: PLAN OF SONDAGE PHASE IV.3.

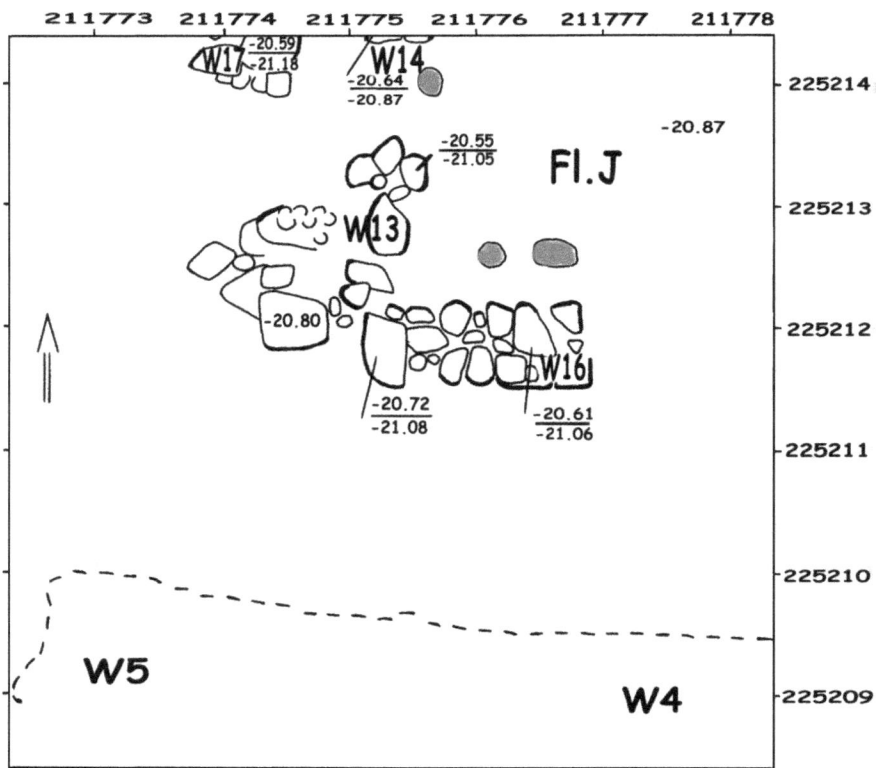

FIG. 2.13 TALL ZAR^{C}A: PLAN OF SONDAGE PHASE IV.3.

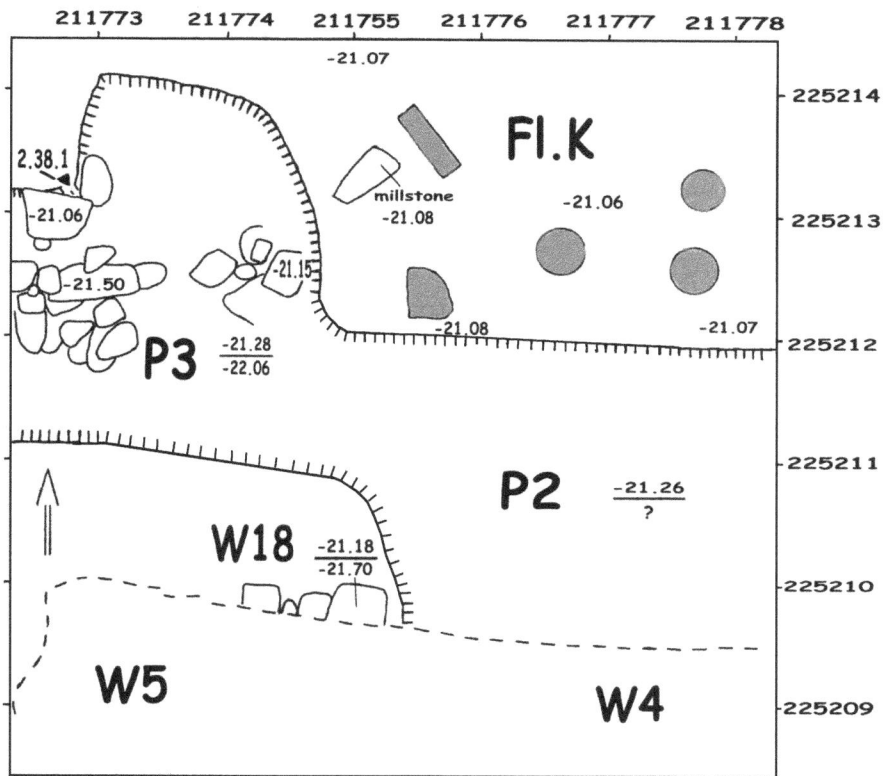

FIG. 2.14 TALL ZAR^{C}A: PLAN OF SONDAGE PHASES IV.4–IV.5.

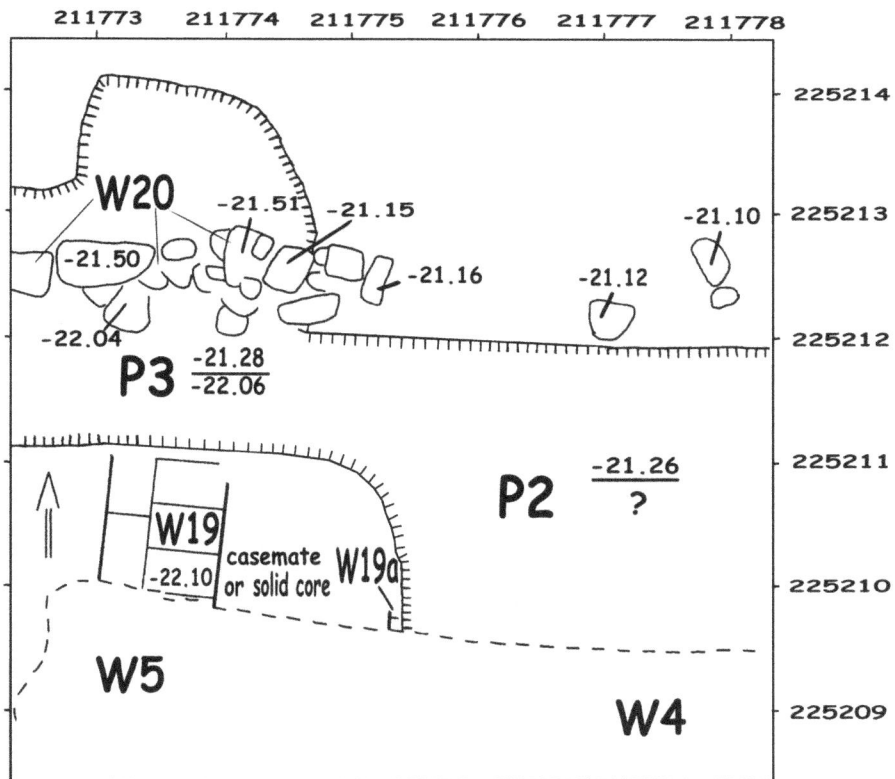

FIG. 2.15 TALL ZAR^{C}A: PLAN OF SONDAGE PHASES V.1–V.2.

211772　211773　211774　211775　211776　211777　211778

west

east

-18

-19

W1

W6

Fl.A

W2

W7

W12

Fl.E

Fl.F

Fl.G

-20

Wz?

FIG. 2.16 TALL ZAR^{C}A: NORTH SECTION OF SONDAGE (2001).

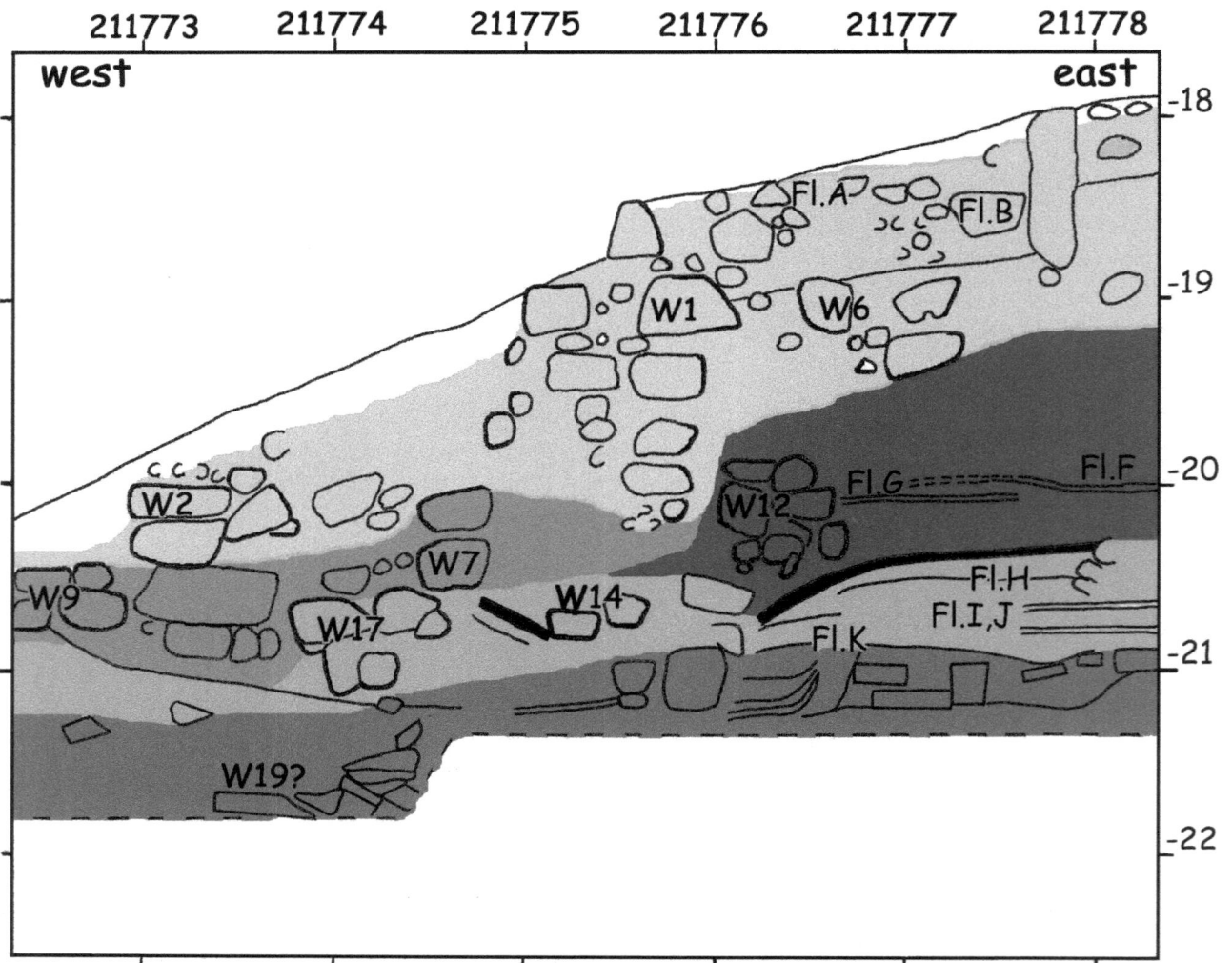

211773　211774　211775　211776　211777　211778

west

east

-18

Fl.A

Fl.B

W1

W6

-19

W2

W7

W14

W12

Fl.G

Fl.F

-20

W9

W17

Fl.H

Fl.I,J

Fl.K

-21

W19?

-22

FIG. 2.17 TALL ZAR^{C}A: NORTH SECTION OF SONDAGE (2002).

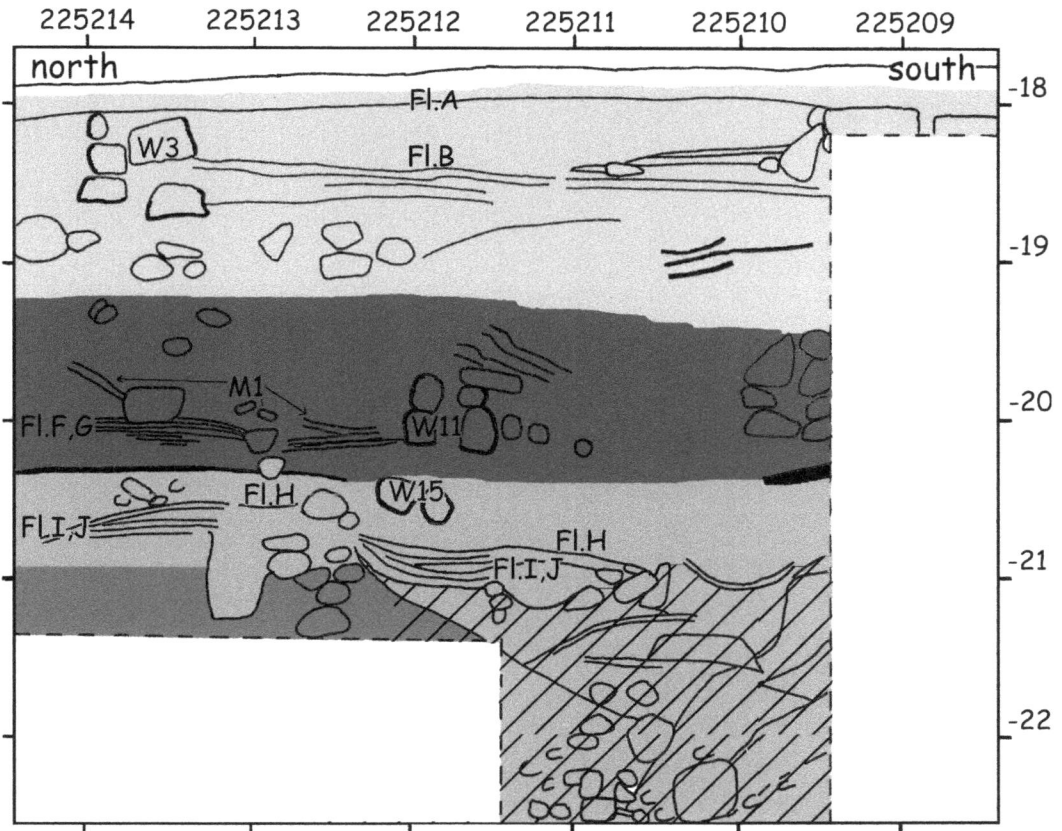

FIG. 2.18 TALL ZAR^CA: EAST SECTION OF SONDAGE.

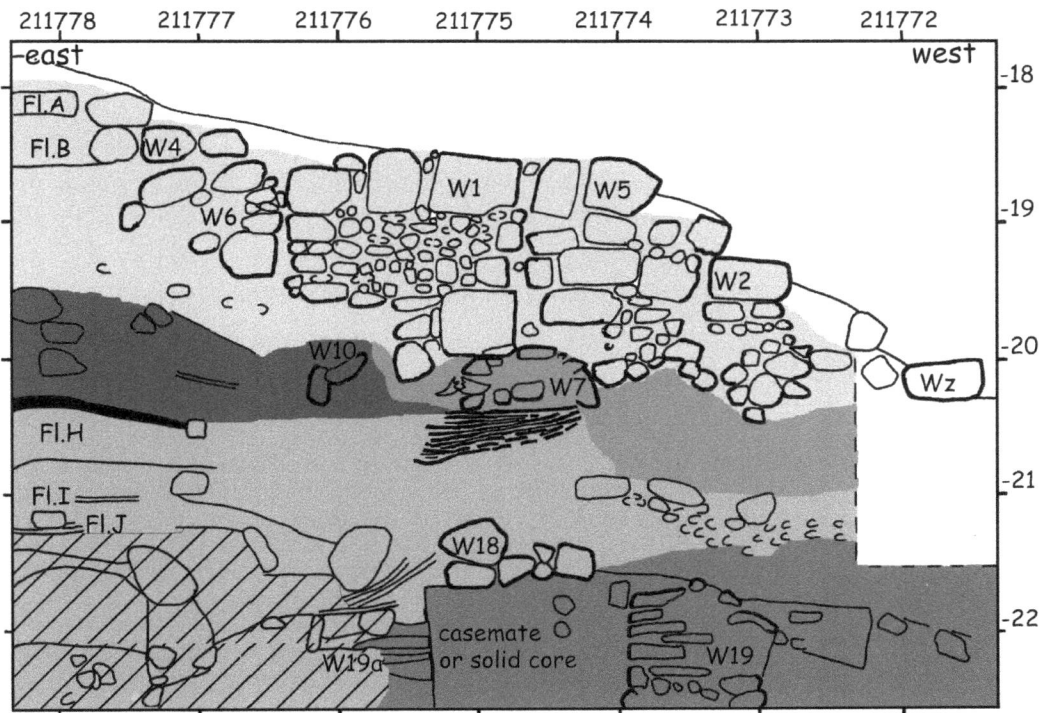

FIG. 2.19: TALL ZAR^CA: SOUTH SECTION OF SONDAGE.

ɔndage Tall Zar'a 2001/2002

Islamic Period

Stratum I phase I.1-2

phase I.3-4

Roman-Byzantine Period

Stratum II phase II.1

phase II.2

Iron Age IIB

Stratum III phase III.1-3

Iron Age I A/B-IIA

Stratum IV phase IV 1-2

Stratum IV phase IV.3a

Stratum IV phase IV.3b

Stratum IV phase IV.4-5

Iron Age IA- Late Bronze Age

Stratum V phase V. 1-2

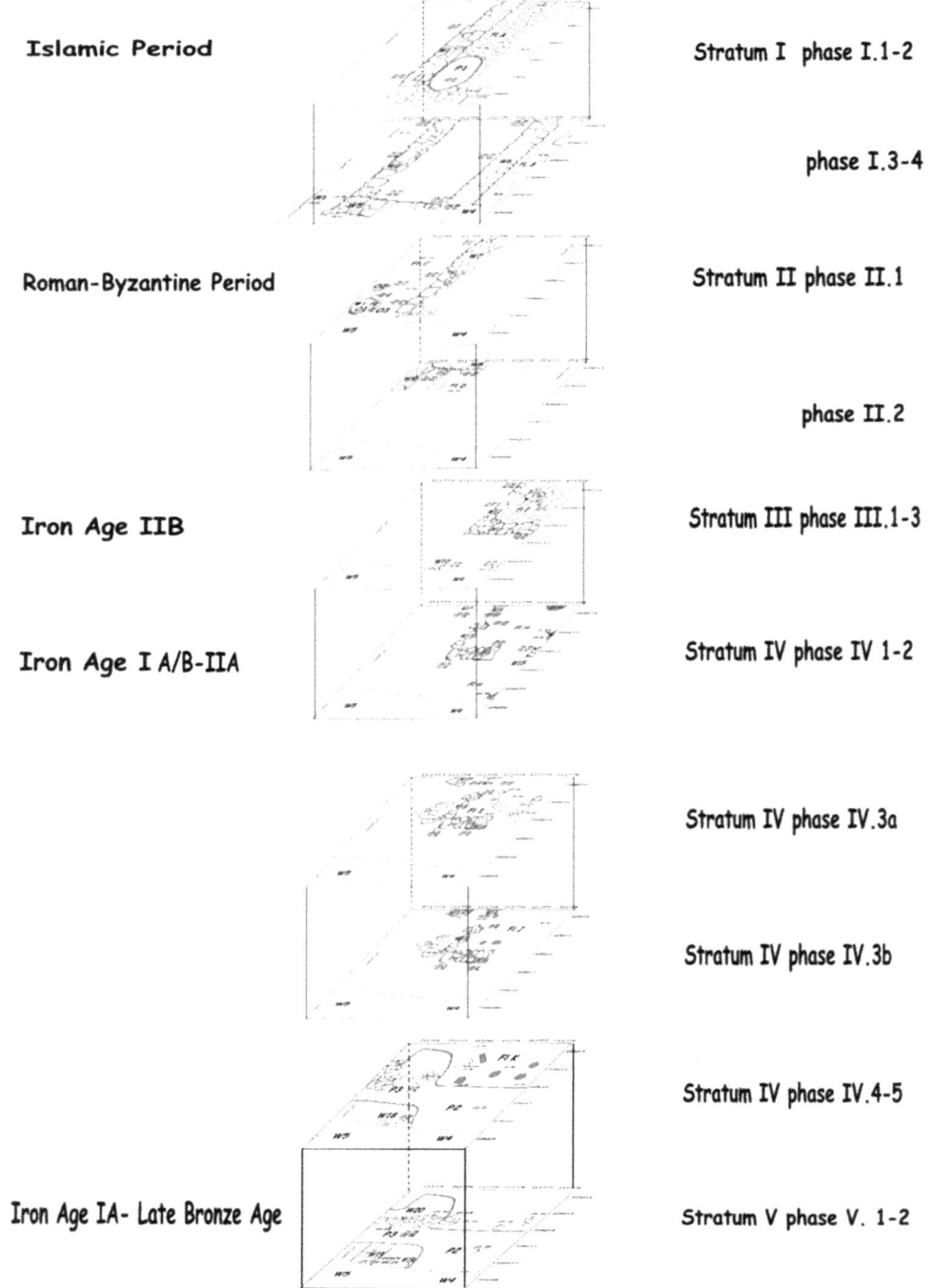

FIG. 2.20 TALL ZAR^{c}A: PHASE PLANS SUPERIMPOSED.

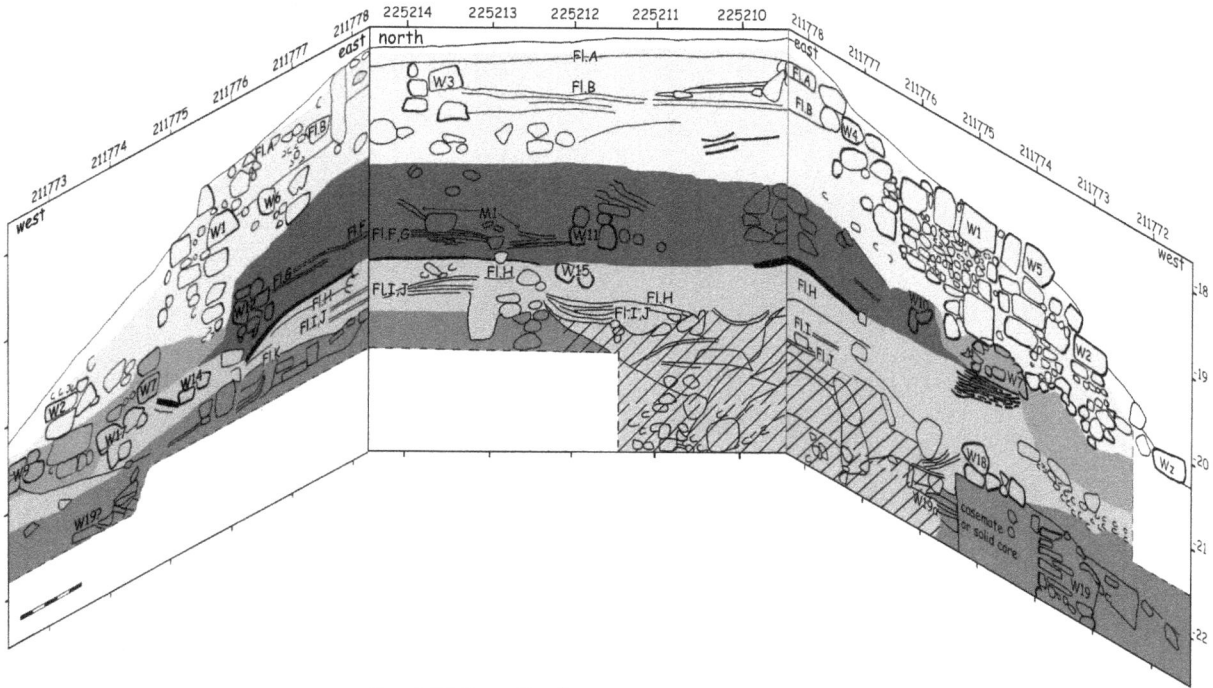

FIG. 2.21 TALL ZAR^{c}A: SECTIONS IN PERSPECTIVE.

FIG. 2.22: PHASE I.2-3 (WALLS W1 AND W6; FLOOR FL.B)

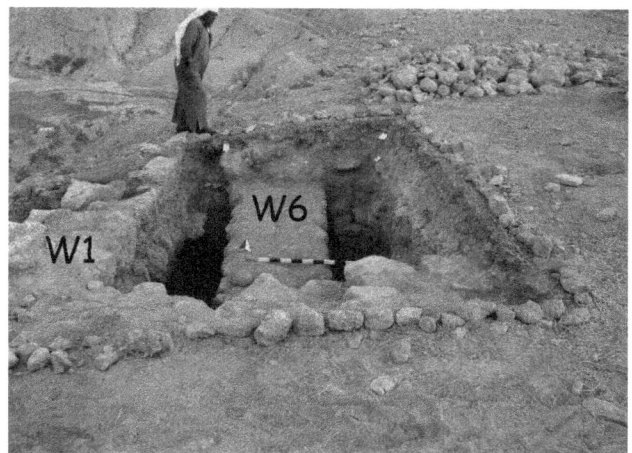

FIG. 2.23: PHASE I.2-3 (WALLS W1 AND WALL 6)

FIG. 2.24: PHASES I.4- II.1 (WALLS W2, Wz; OVENS O1,O2)

FIG. 2.25: PHASE I.4-II.1 (WALLS W2, W7; FLOOR FL.C; OVENS O1, O2)

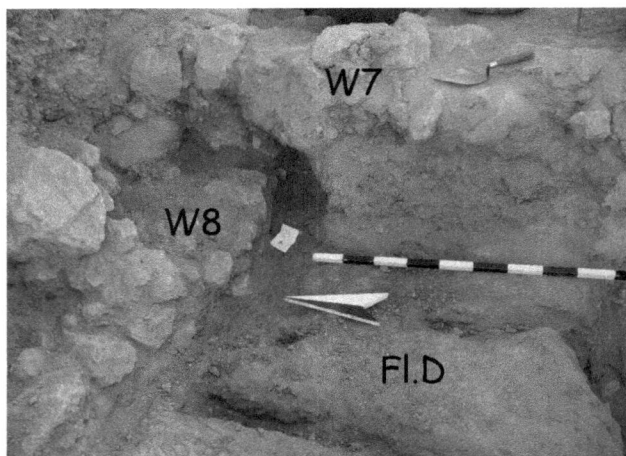

FIG. 2.26: PHASE II.1-2 (WALLS W7, W8; FLOOR Fl.D)

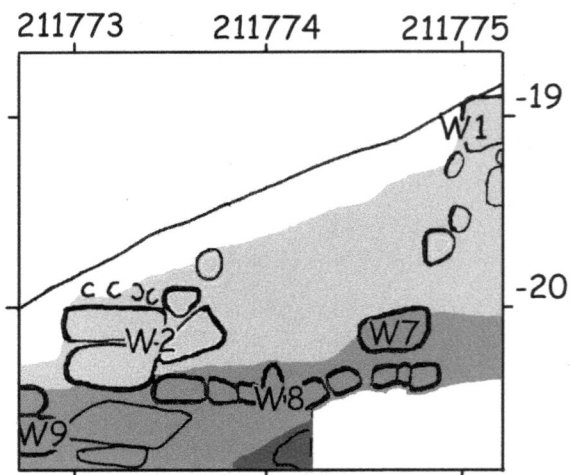

FIG. 2.27: PHASE I.4; II.1-2 (WALLS W2, W7, W8, W9)

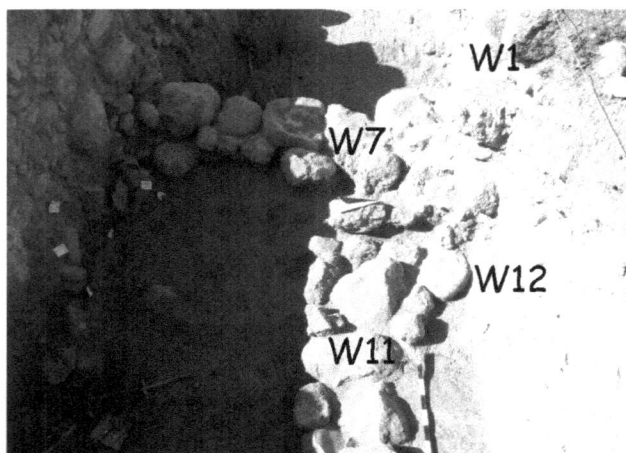

FIG.2.28: PHASE II.1, III.2 (WALLS W7, W11, W12)

FIG. 2.29 EARLY 2002-CAMPAIGN. VIEW OF STRATA I-III (WALLS W1, W2, W6, W7, W11)

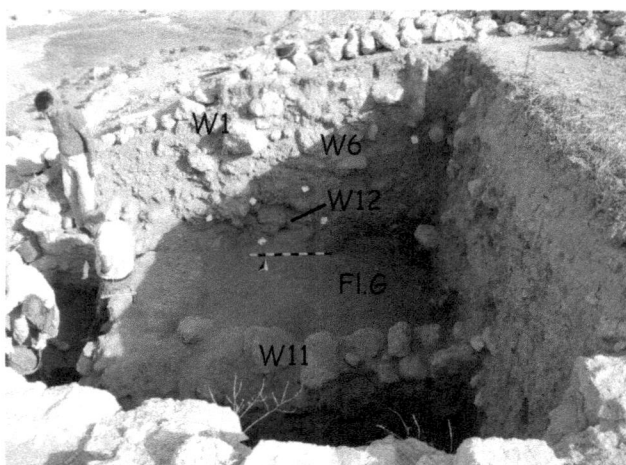

FIG. 2.30: PHASE III.2 (WALLS W11, W12; FLOOR Fl.G)

FIG. 2.31 PHASE IV.3 (WALLS W13, W14, W16; FLOOR Fl.I)

FIG. 2.32: PHASE IV.3 (WALLS W13, W14, W16; FLOOR FL.J)

FIG. 2.33: PHASE IV.3-5 (WALLS W13, W16, W17; FLOORS FL.J, FL.K; PIT P3)

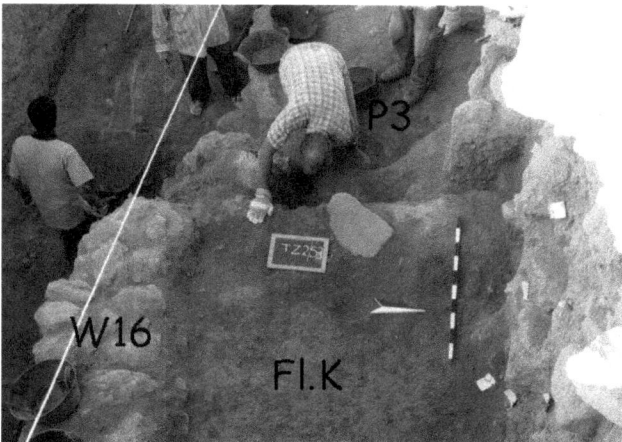

FIG. 2.34: PHASE IV.3-5 (WALL W16; FLOOR FL.K; PIT P3)

FIG. 2.35: PHASE IV.5; V.2 (WALLS W18, W19, W19A)

FIG. 2.36: END OF 2002-CAMPAIGN. GENERAL VIEW OF NORTH SECTION.

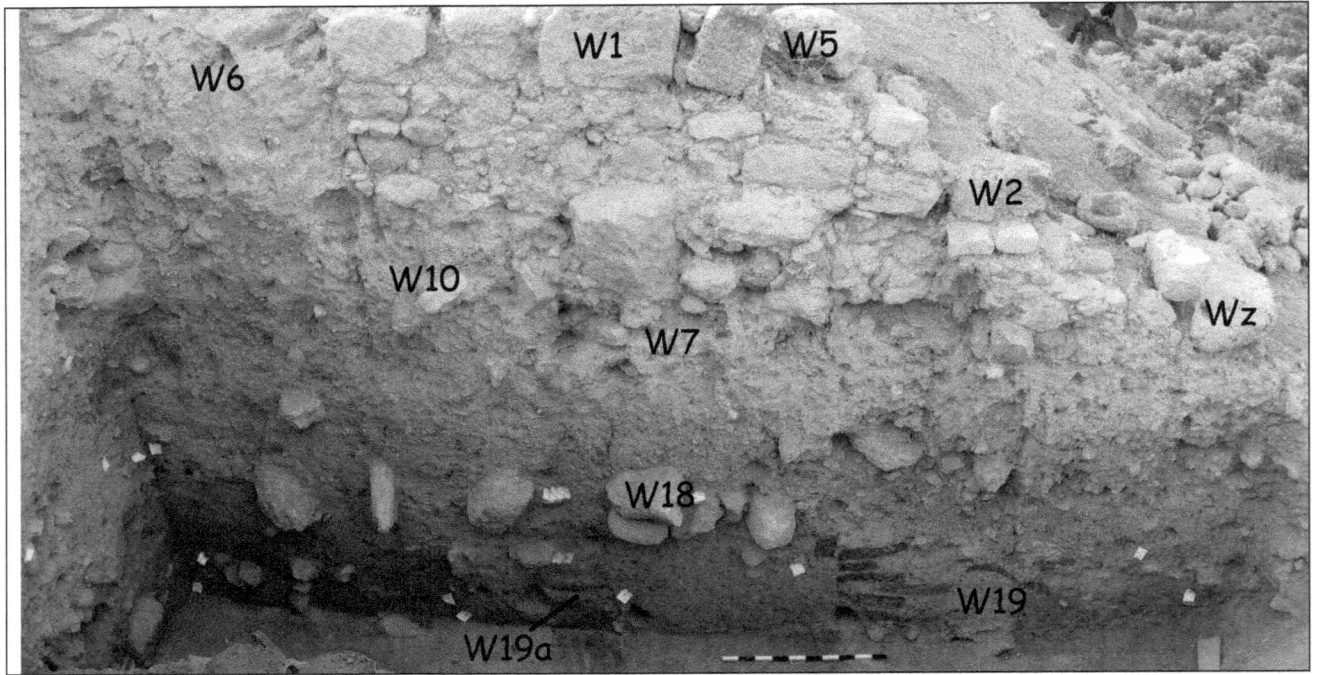

FIG. 2.37 GENERAL VIEW OF SOUTH SECTION. END OF 2002-CAMPAIGN.

CHAPTER 3

In general, the N–S walls in the area run NNE (Walls W1, W2, W6, W7, W9, W12, W13, W19 and Wz), following the curvature of west side of the tell and the E–W walls run roughly WNW (Walls W4, W5, W8, W11 and W20; Fig. 2.6–2.15). The area of the sondage is too limited for general conclusions about the layout of houses. However, some observations on the buildings and the use of the excavated spaces can be made. Remarkable was that installations and utensils for food preparation are found on most of the floors discovered in Strata II–IV.

3.1 Stratum I, Phases 2–4.

The remains of the Early Islamic Period divide at least two building phases. The latest is Phase I.2 (Fig. 2.6): Wall W1 with a cobblestone floor to the east and flagstones on the south side of the trench (Floor Fl.A), on the eastern side cobbles are missing. The solidity of this wall and its facing west gives the impression that this was a retaining wall. The floor was destroyed by Pit P1 dug later.

The earlier Phase I.3 (Fig. 2.7) has a similar layout to the former. However, the N–S Wall W6 was situated further east and two E–W walls (Walls W3 and W4) were visible. Wall W2, N–S, and Wall W5, E–W, may also have belonged to Phase I.3 making two walls of a room, but traces of any relation to Wall W6 had been erased by intrusion of the later Wall W1. Like Wall W1, the earlier Walls W6 and W2 faced west so that they must have been retaining walls, each supporting a terrace, of which the one east of Wall W6 was higher up the slope and had its successive pavements preserved. The present information was insufficient to establish whether this floor was open to air or roofed over.

3.2 Stratum II, Phases 1–2.

Remains from the Late Roman/Early Byzantine Period were found in the western part of the sondage. To the later Phase II.1 belong Plaster Floor Fl.C and N–S Wall W7, the west side of which was constructed of ashlars and boulders, while its east side was mainly of field stones and cobbles (Fig. 2.8). Probably, Wall W7 was a retaining wall with only the western face exposed. West of Wall W7 was an area for food preparation, as the remains of three *tanānīr*, many *tannūr* sherds, some charcoal blocks and a "sling stone" (for grinding?) on Floor Fl.C indicate. The remains of one complete, though smashed, cooking pot inside *tannūr* Oven O1, indicates that these ovens were used also for other purposes than baking bread.

From the earlier Phase II.2 was Plaster Floor Fl.D on which were also many *tannūr* sherds and two "sling stones" (perhaps again for grinding) and Walls W8 and W9 bordering Floor Fl.D on the N and on the W. However there were no traces of walls to the E or to the S (Fig. 2.9).

About the layout of the building in both phases, little can be said. If there were a contemporary room east of Wall W7 in Phase II.1 or II.2, its floor was lying on a higher level than Floor Fl.C. Any traces of such a floor were, however, erased by later building activities from the Stratum I. Since walls of Ovens O1–O3 were discovered still standing partly or almost complete, they were in use side by side during the later phase, before the building was abandoned – there was no indication of destruction of Phase II.1. Several ovens together in one room also have been found in Roman–Byzantine remains at other sites. However more information is needed on the distribution of baking installations from a larger excavated area on the tell to draw any conclusion about the baking and cooking routine and about the social situation of the inhabitants.[1] In Phase II.2, the many *tannūr* sherds indicated that the area of Floor Fl.D was also used for baking and cooking.

3.3 Stratum III, Phase 2.

Walls W11 (E–W) and W12 (N–S), and the assumed Wall W10 (N–S) constituted the remains of an Iron Age IIB house with at least two rooms, or a room and a courtyard. The upper floor Floor Fl.E consisting of cobble stones covered with a thin loamy layer was found only between Walls W11 and W12 (Fig. 2.10), besides the complete chalice, there were many *tannūr* sherds on it. The lower Floors Fl.F and Fl.G associated with these walls contained gravel. Larger and smaller areas of these floors were excavated in the eastern half of the sondage. These constructions had been built after a deposit of reddish earth accumulated on a thick layer of ash had covered and sealed the remains of the earlier strata / phases.

3.4 Stratum IV, Phase 2.

Remains of the latest house of Stratum IV (Iron IA/B–IIA) were visible in E–W Walls W15 and W16, and in N–S Walls W13, W14 and W17. The remains on the associated Floor Fl.H, found between Walls W13-W17, and S of Wall W15, indicated that also this building had at least two rooms. Moreover, there were two openings in

---

[1] Cf. Reich, 2003, 140–158; Hirschfeld, 1995, 58.

Floor	Stratum, phase	*Tannūr*	*Tannūr* sherds	Ash pit	"Sling stone"	Millstone	Cooking-pot sherds
C	II, 1	xxx	many		x		complete pot
D	II, 2		many		xx		homogeneous
E	III, 2		many		xx	x?	homogeneous
G	III, 2						few
H	IV, 2		few	xxx	xx		complete pots and many sherds
I	IV, 3		very few	x			homogeneous
J	IV, 3			xxx			many
K	IV, 4		many	xxxxx	xxx	x	very many

Table 3.1 Synopsis of floors, *tanānīr* and implements for food preparation.

the walls, between Walls W15 and W16 and between Walls W13 and W14 (Fig. 2.11). There were traces of food preparation in three shallow pits with ash, on each of which a complete cooking pot or cooking-pot sherds, and two "sling stones" (for grinding?). These findings suggest a way of cooking and baking different from that on Floors Fl.C, Fl.D and Fl.E, where only *tannūr* remains were found. The complete cooking pot found *in situ* on the ash (Fig 2.11: TZ 2.33; Fig 4.7:9) indicates that the building was evacuated, with the household utensils left in place, and that the area was not demolished afterwards.

3.5 Stratum IV, Phase 3

In the earlier phase of Stratum IV, the plan of the house was the same as in Phase IV.2. Of its Floor I (Fig. 2.12), there were also patches discovered S of Wall W16. Between Walls W16 and W13 was a stone circle with ash inside, which may have been a hearth or a silo. The lower floor of this phase, Floor Fl.J, like Floor Fl.H, had three shallow pits filled with ash (Fig. 2.13).

3.6 Stratum IV, Phase 4

In the earliest phase of Stratum IV, there were no traces of walls. In the NE quarter of the sondage on Floor Fl.K were five shallow pits with ash, many *tannūr* sherds, a large mill-stone and three "sling stones" (for grinding?) (Fig. 2.14). The lack of walls indicates a building plan different from the later Phases IV,3, IV,2 and III,2. The number of ash pits suggested that the area in this phase might have been open to the air, possibly a courtyard. It was not clear how far Floor Fl.K extended southwards and westwards. Its remains may have vanished, sliding down into the sinking soil of the large Pits P3 and P2 S of the retaining Wall W20 (see below 3.7). In the S section were the remains of two layers of boulders with the remains of floors to its side, which may perhaps be of Floor K. These boulders may be the remains of a N–S wall, tentatively Wall W18, cut by the large Pit P3–P2.

3.7 Stratum V, Phase 1

The E–W line of boulders discovered in the centre of Pit P3 may have been the remains of Wall W20. This area of the sondage was not excavated to a level deep enough to draw conclusions about building remains related to this line of stones (Fig. 2.15). Since yellowish loamy soil was found on the N side as far as this line of stones and the greyish-reddish soil of Pits P2–P3 had built up against its S side, this wall might have been a retaining wall built to retain the loamy soil on the N.

3.8 Stratum V, Phase 2

Pit P3 intersected the remains of a double N–S wall made of mud bricks on a foundation of layers of field stones (Wall W19) and gravel (Wall W19a) (Fig. 2.15). The space between the two was solidly packed with loamy soil. It is not clear whether this was done on purpose or whether it resulted from deterioration of Walls W19/W19a. The excavated area was too limited to draw any conclusion about the building to which these walls belonged.

3.9 Conclusion

All the floors excavated bore remains of food preparation. The data add little or nothing to our knowledge of the layout or construction of the houses in our area. Rooms or floors with ovens may have been open to the air or sheltered with some kind of roofing.[2] Roman–Byzantine remains of baking and cooking utensils are usually found in courtyards,[3] though they can also occur in covered areas on the ground floor of buildings.[4] As for the Iron Age I, baking and cooking utensils are found in rooms and in open spaces (courtyards, streets) as well,[5] the same as for Iron Age II.[6]

---

[2] Cf. McQuitty, 1984, 261-262; idem, 1993, 60, 63, 73; Mulder-Hijmans, 2008, 211–230. See for the problem of the escape of smoke from ovens and the need to have them located in a roofed or an unroofed space Pritchard, 1985, 29-30; Netzer, 1992, 195-199.
[3] Hirschfeld, 1995, 31–34, 58, 274, 290.
[4] Hirschfeld, 1995, 264.
[5] Fritz and Kempinski, 1983, 108, Plates 13B (courtyard), 74B (room), 76B (room), 77A–B (rooms), 77C–D (courtyards).
[6] Chambon, 1984, 37–38; Yadin, 1962, Plates VII 3,5 (rooms), XVII 1,4 (courtyard); Briend and Humbert, 1980, 29, 32f., 158: Fig. 43.

CHAPTER 4

This chapter begins with a survey of the ceramic finds, which is intended to present an overall – though not exhaustive – picture of the pottery excavated in the sondage. In Fig. 4.1–4.8, examples of pottery types are arranged from the latest (Mediaeval Islamic) to the earliest (Middle Bronze IIC). The contribution of these finds to the stratigraphic analysis will become evident in Chap. 9, Conclusions.

Some elements of the pottery are discussed in two excurses in the second part of this chapter, while Chapter 7 will present statistical studies of the repertoire.

4.1: Mediaeval–Late Roman pottery

Fig.4.1	Description (date)	Phase
4.1:1	Handmade geometrical painted ware: bi-ansulate jug (12th-17th cent.)[1]	surface
4.1:2	Bowl: sgraffito and gouge-decorated; transparent yellow glaze over a cream-coloured slib, interior and exterior (iron oxide; 13th-14th cent.)[2]	surface
4.1:3	Bowl: monochrome slip-glazed; transparent glaze with green patches (copper oxide; 13th-14th cent.)[3]	surface
4.1:4	Late Byzantine jar: shoulder and neck (6th -early 7th cent.).[4]	surface
4.1:5	Late Roman basin: rim (3rd-4th cent.).[5]	I.2
4.1:6	Late Roman basin: rim (3rd-4th cent.).[6]	I.2
4.1:7	Byzantine-Umayyad bowl: complete profile (6th-8th cent.).[7]	I.1-I.3
4.1:8	Late Roman C Ware, Form 3F: rim (6th cent.).[8]	I.3
4.1:9	Late Roman-Early Byzantine jar: Rim and neck (3rd-4th cent.).[9]	I.2
4.1:10	Idem	I.2
4.1:11	Idem	I.2
4.1:12	Cooking bowl, single groove in the rim exterior (late1st-late 3rd cent.).[10]	surface
4.1:13	Cooking bowl, two grooves in the rim exterior (late 1st/early 2nd-mid 4th cent.).[11]	surface
4.1:14	Cooking bowl, bulge at rim interior, occasional knob or tiny loop handle (mid 3rd-early 5th cent.).[12]	surface
4.1:15	Idem	surface
4.1:16	Cooking bowl, base (mid 3rd-early 5th cent.).[13]	I.2

4.2: Late Roman/Early Byzantine-Hellenistic pottery

Fig.4.2	Description (date)	Phase
4.2:1	Late Roman-Early Byzantine cooking pot: bi-ansulate, short neck (2nd-4th cent.).[14]	II.1
4.2:2	Cooking pot, wide opening, a wide groove on the broad horizontal to slightly upturned rim, loop handles, rounded profile of widest circumference (mid 1st cent. BCE-mid 2nd cent. CE).[15]	II.1
4.2:3	Like previous, but sharp carination on widest circumference (early 2nd-late 4th cent. CE).[16]	I.2

---

[1] Smith, 1973, 240, Pl. 73:24; Franken and Kalsbeek, 1975, 167-199; LaGro, 2002, 55-57, Pl. 70:3.41; Hirschfeld, 1997, 386-388, Pl.II:1; Ziadeh, 1995, 226-227, Fig.7: 1-3.

[2] Hirschfeld, 1997, 393-394, Pl. IV:9-12; Pringle, 1985, 183-186, Fig. 6:37-38; Pringle, 1984, 103-104, Fig. 7:55.

[3] Hirschfeld, 1997, 390-392, Pl. III: 16-20; Pringle, 1985, 177-178, Fig. 3:13; Pringle, 1984, 102-103, Fig. 7:41-47.

[4] Smith and Day, 1989, 107, Pl. 48:8; 52:12; McNicoll et al., 1992, 147, Pl. 98:7; Loffreda,1974, 43-44, Fig.8:3.

[5] Hirschfeld, 1997, 350,352, Pl. II:4; Weiss, 2005, 286, 282 Pl. CIII:13; McNicoll et al.,1992, 170,171, Pl. 108:9.

[6] Hirschfeld, 1997, 350,352, Pl. II:14; Weiss, 2005, 286, 282 Pl. CIII:13.

[7] Hirschfeld, 1997, 361,366, Pl. VIII:11.

[8] Hirschfeld, 1997, 359,364, Pl. VII:11; Hayes, 1972, 333-335, 338; McNicoll et al., 1992, 174, Pl. 110:15.

[9] Hirschfeld, 1997, 351,358, Pl. IV: 2-3,10; McNicoll et al., 1992,139,170-171, Pl. 92:4; 108:1-3; Weiss, 2005, 279-281, Pl. CII: 2,3,5.

[10] Adan-Bayewitz, 1993, 88-91 (Type 1A); Weiss, 2005, 287, 284, Pl. C.IV:9.

[11] Adan-Bayewitz, 1993, 91-97 (Type 1B); Hirschfeld, 1997, 348-349,357, Pl. I:1-9;VI:7; Weiss, 2005, 287,284, Pl. C.IV:10; McNicoll et al.,1992, 135, Pl.92:2.

[12] Adan-Bayewitz, 1993, 103-109 (Type 1E); Weiss, 2005, 287,284, Pl. C.IV:12; Hirschfeld, 1997, 357,362, Pl. VI:9,12; McNicoll et al.,1992, 170, Pl.108:14.

[13] Adan-Bayewitz, 1993, 88,98-109 (Type 1C-E); Hirschfeld, 1997, 348-348, Pl. I:12; Weiss, 2005, 287, 284, Pl. C.IV:12.

[14] Hirschfeld, 1997, 351, 354, Pl. III:24; McNicoll et al., 1982, 84, 144-145, Pl. 132:10; Fischer, 1993, 289-290.

[15] Adan-Bayewitz, 1993, 111-119 (Type 3A); Weiss, 2005, 277-278,284, 287 Pl. C.I:5; C.IV:7.

[16] Adan-Bayewitz,,1993, 119-124 (Type 3B); Weiss, 2005, 287,284, 293, 290, Pl. C.IV:8; C.VI:14.

4.2:4	Cooking jug (early Roman?)	II.1
4.2:5	Cooking pot, slightly splaying neck, groove on interior just below rim top (mid 1st cent. BCE – mid 2[n] cent. CE).[17]	II.1
4.2:6	Roman rouletted ware (1st-2nd cent. CE).[18]	II.1
4.2:7	Eastern Terra Sigillata Form 11-12 (late 1st cent. BCE-1st cent. CE?).[19]	surface
4.2:8	Idem	I.4
4.2:9	Hellenistic black glazed ware: base with ring foot (2nd cent. BCE).[20]	II.2
4.2:10	Roman glass bowl (1st-3rd cent. CE).[21]	I.4

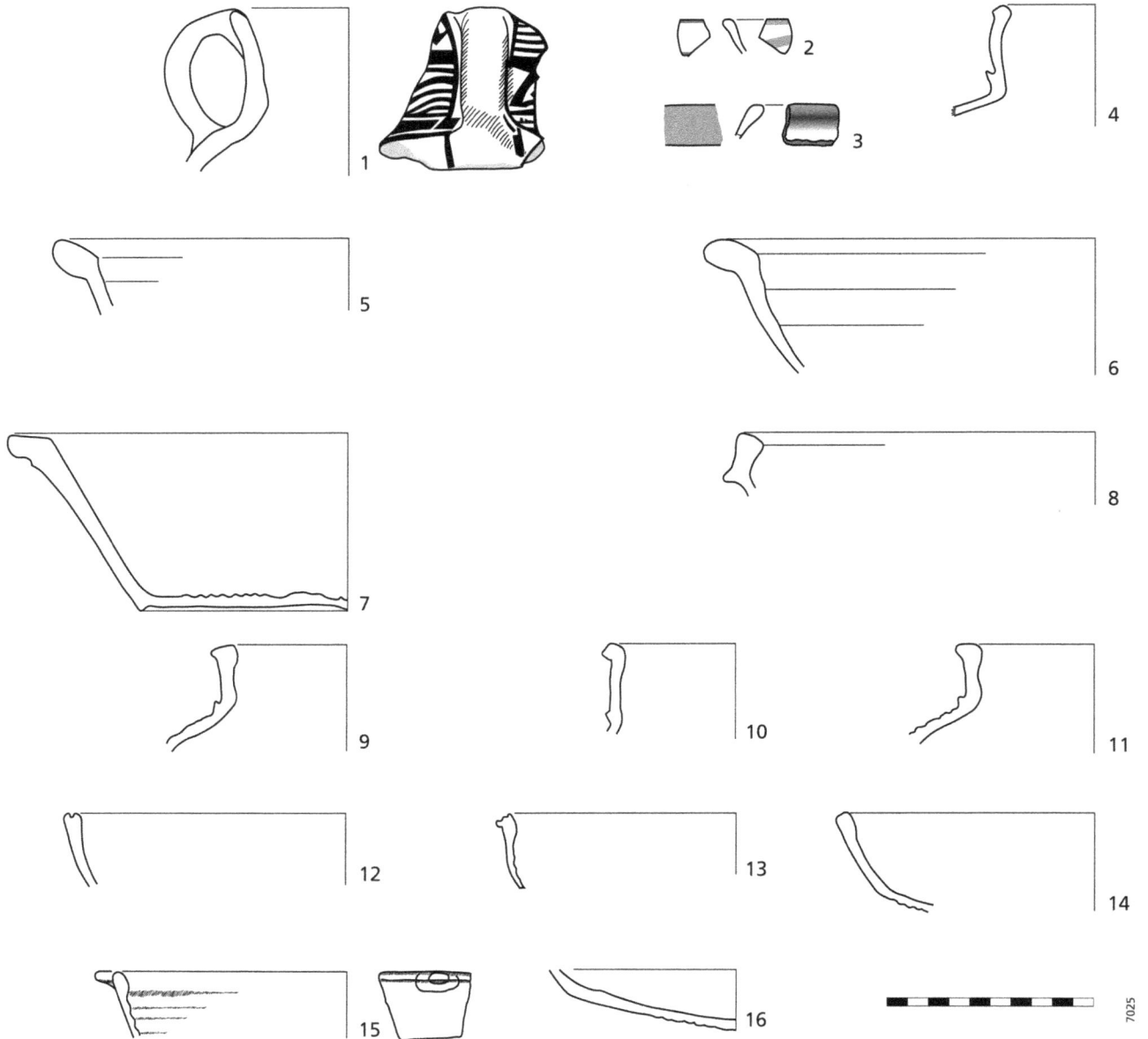

FIG. 4.1: MEDIAEVAL–LATE ROMAN POTTERY

---

[17] Adan-Bayewitz, 1993, 124-125 (Type 4A).

[18] Crowfoot et al., 1957, 340-342, Fig. 82:3.

[19] Crowfoot et al., 1957, 310,329-330: Fig. 79:5-6, dated Form 11 in late 1st cent. BCE and Form 12 in 2nd-3rd cent. CE; however, Gunneweg et al., 1983, 86, 104; Fig. 21:6, combined both and dated 88 BCE-50 CE.

[20] Crowfoot et al., 1957, 220-224; McNicoll et al., 1982, 70 (Text); 136, Pl. 128:1-7 (Plates and Illustrations).

[21] Isings, 1957, 59 (Form 43); Dussart, 1998, 59,243, Pl.3 (BI.1322a); McNicoll et al., 1982,, 84-87,144-147, Pl. 132:1,9;133:7; McNicoll et al., 1992, 127, Pl. 87:7.

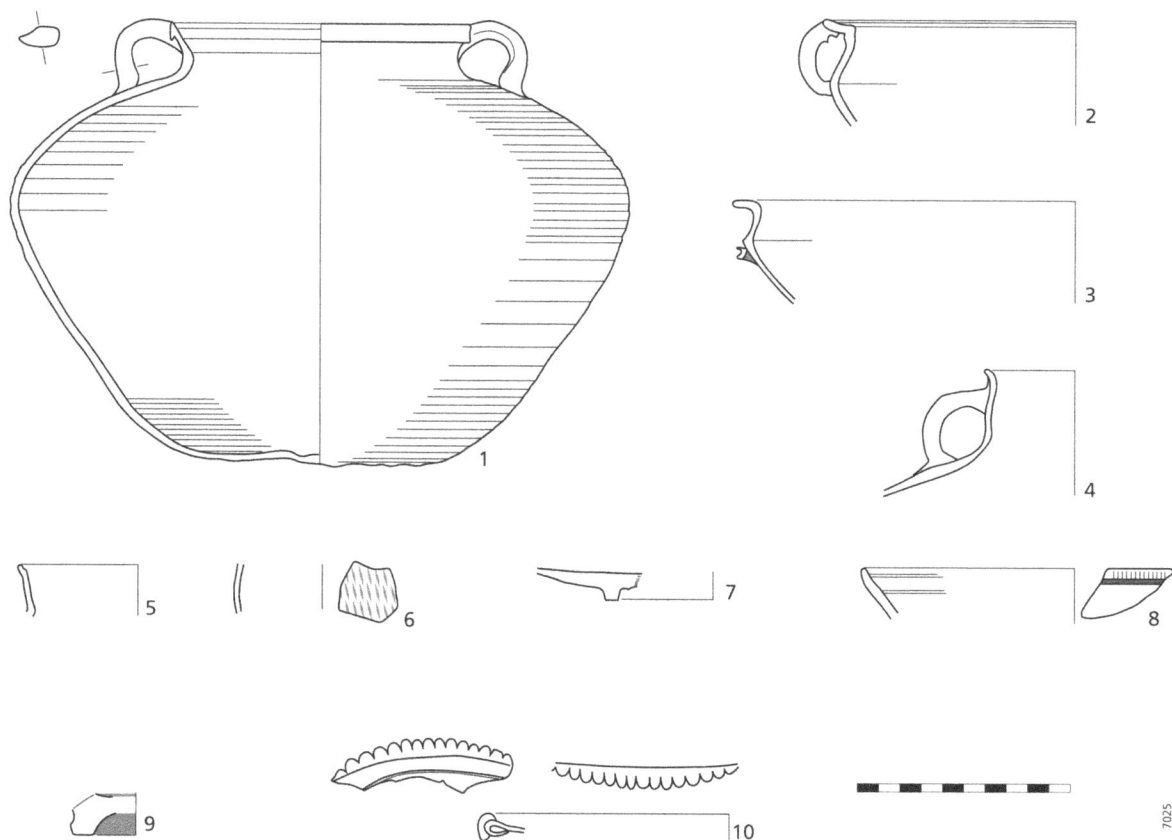

FIG. 4.2: LATE ROMAN/EARLY BYZANTINE-HELLENISTIC POTTERY

4.3: Iron Age I-IIC pottery

Fig.4.3	Description (date)	Phase
4.3:1	Flat base, shaped by scraping away surplus clay. (IA IIB) [22]	IV.1
4.3:2	Rounded base, finished after it was cut from the clay cone. Juglet (IA IIB-C) [23]	III.1
4.3:3	Rounded base, thrown closed upside down. Juglet. (IA IIB-C) [24]	surface/IV.3
4.3:4	Bowl, raised flat base (IA IIB) [25]	IV.5 (P2a)
4.3:5	Bowl, burnished inside, ring burnished outside. (IA IIA-B) [26]	IV.1
4.3:6	Chalice, foot made separately. (IA I-IIB) [27]	IV.5 (P2a)
4.3:7	Chalice, foot made separately. (IA I-IIB) [28]	III.1
4.3:8	Crater. (IA I-IIA) [29]	II.2
4.3:9	Crater. (IA I-IIA) [30]	IV.5 (P2a)
4.3:10	Pyxis, handle. (IA IIA-B) [31]	IV.1
4.3:11	Juglet. (IA I-IIC) [32]	I.2
4.3:12	Juglet. (IA IIA) [33]	IV.5 (P2a)
4.3:13	Jug, imitation "double-handle". (IA IIC) [34]	III.1

[22] Franken and Steiner, 1990, 92-93, fig. 5-6:5.
[23] Amiran, 1969, Pl. 87:9-13; 88:16-18; Pritchard, 1985, Fig.7:5-13.
[24] Franken and Steiner, 1990, 93-94.
[25] Franken and Steiner, 1990, fig. 2-14:4,5; 2-15:4,6,7; 2-21C:155;2-23:3,4;2-24:2,3.
[26] Amiran, 1969, 201, 206; Franken, 1974, 93, 124.
[27] Amiran, 1969, Pl. 68:1-13; McNicoll *et al.*, 1992., Pl. 68:4; Franken and Kalsbeek, 1969, Fig. 55:17; 61:34; 63:23,24,28; 69:28; Rast, 1978, Fig. 27:2; 53:5; 69:3,5.
[28] Cf. previous footnote.
[29] Amiran, 1969, Pl. 71:1; McNicoll *et al.*, 1992, Pl.49:11;52:6; Franken and Kalsbeek, 1969, Fig. 59:111-113; Rast, 1978, Fig. 4:8; Vilders, 1992, Fig. 5:40-42, 197; McGovern, 1986, Fig. 51:24.
[30] Amiran, 1969, Pl. 70:3;71:6; Franken and Kalsbeek, 1969, Fig. 75:92; McGovern, 1986, Fig. 51:27.
[31] Amiran, 1969, Pl. 96: 16,17,19-24.
[32] Amiran, 1969, Pl. 86:12; 88:19; 89:22; Franken and Kalsbeek, 1969, Fig. 70:51.
[33] Amiran, 1969, Pl. 86:13 (cf. 86:6; 88:13).
[34] Amiran, 1969, Pl. 88:3-4.

4.3:14	Jug. Painted bands, not slipped. (IA IIA) [35]	I.2
4.3:15	Jug. (IA I-IIA) [36]	I.3
4.3:16	Jar. (IA I) [37]	III.2
4.3:17	Jar. (IA I-IIA) [38]	I.3
4.3:18	Jar, handle with rounded imprint. (IA I-IIA/C) [39]	III.1
4.3:19	Jar, monochrome painted bands, not slipped. (IA I) [40]	III.1/III.3/IV.5(P2a)

4.4: Iron Age I pottery

Fig.4.4	Description (date)	Phase
4.4:1	Thin walled bowl. (IA IA) [41]	IV.5 (P2a)
4.4:2	Shallow bowl. (IA I) [42]	IV.5 (P2a)
4.4:3	Large bowl. (IA I) [43]	surface/IV.3
4.4:4	Bowl. (IA I) [44]	IV.2
4.4:5	Bowl. (IA I) [45]	IV.3
4.4:6	Bowl. (IA-I) [46]	IV.4
4.4:7	Bowl. (IA I) [47]	IV.4
4.4:8	Deep Bowl. (IA I) [48]	IV.4
4.4:9	Bowl. (IA I) [49]	II.2
4.4:10	Bowl. (IA I) [50]	IV.4
4.4:11	Jar. (IA I) [51]	I.3
4.4:12	Jar. (IA I) [52]	I.4
4.4:13	Jar. (IA I) [53]	IV.3
4.4:14	Jar. (IA I) [54]	IV.3
4.4:15	Crater. (IA I) [55]	IV.3
4.4:16	Jar. Painted bands, not slipped. (IA I) [56]	III.3
4.4:17	Jar. Painted bands, not slipped. (IA I) [57]	IV.4
4.4:18	Jarhandle. Painted crossing bands. Not slipped. (IA I) [58]	IV.2
4.4:19	Jug/pilgrims bottle? Painted bands. Not slipped. (IA I) [59]	surface/IV.3
4.4:20	Collared Rim Jar (IA I) [60]	IV.5 (P3)
4.4:21	Collared Rim Jar, body sherd with handle (IA I) [61]	IV.5 (P3)
4.4:22	Collared Rim Jar. (IA I) [62]	surface
4.4:23	Shoulder Collared Rim Jar. (IA I) [63]	I.2
4.4:24	Lamp. (IA I) [64]	IV.3

[35] McNicoll *et al.*, 1982, Fig.62:8; Rast, 1978, Fig. 40:8.

[36] McNicoll *et al.*, 1992, Pl.52:12,13; Franken and Kalsbeek, 1969, Fig. 54:106-107; 51:13-15; 54:101-102; 57:29; 60:4,7; 76:50-51; Rast, 1978, Fig. 55:1.

[37] McNicoll *et al.*, 1992, Pl.64:11; 65:5,9; Franken and Kalsbeek, 1969, Fig. 54:122; Rast, 1978, Fig. 20:3.

[38] Franken and Kalsbeek, 1969, Fig. 57:37; 60:21-22; 62:17; Rast, 1978, Fig. 11:3; 22:3; 24:3.

[39] Amiran, 1969, Pl. 78:1-4; Rast, 1978, Fig. 10:12-14; 88:2.

[40] Amiran, 1969, Pl. 78:1-4; Franken and Kalsbeek, 1969, 172-174, Fig. 51:58,63,64; 52:1; 55:11; 65:60; McNicoll *et al.*,1982, Pl.122:14.

[41] Franken and Kalsbeek, 1969, Fig. 46:36; 50:6,7,9; 60:66; McNicoll *et al.*, 1992, Pl. 52:4-5.

[42] Rast, 1978, Fig. 13:7-9.

[43] Franken and Kalsbeek, 1969, Fig. 46:39; 71:82-83,85,91.

[44] Franken and Kalsbeek, 1969, Fig. 59:95; McNicoll *et al.*, 1982, Pl.120:12; McGovern, 1986, Fig. 55:61; Rast, 1978, Fig. 89:4-5.

[45] Franken and Kalsbeek, 1969, Fig. 57:17; 59:89; 66:73; 75:19; 76:3; McNicoll *et al.*, 1992, Pl.65:1.

[46] Franken and Kalsbeek, 1969, Fig. 50:62-65; 54:89; 64:64,79.

[47] Franken and Kalsbeek, 1969, Fig. 46:60; 67:8; 69:89; 70:9-10; 72:11-14; 75:49-50.

[48] Franken and Kalsbeek, 1969, Fig. 46:19-21; 49:50; 54:10; 56:59; 64:40,44; 74:65,69; 77:6-9,32,34.

[49] Amiran, 1969, Pl. 60:1-3,5; McNicoll *et al.*, 1992, Pl. 52:9.

[50] Amiran, 1969, Pl. 69:2; Franken and Kalsbeek, 1969, Fig. 64:42; Rast, 1978, Fig. 4:8,9;12:1; McNicoll *et al.*, 1992, Pl. 49:11.

[51] Franken and Kalsbeek, 1969, Fig. 50:101; McNicoll *et al.*, 1992, Pl. 52:16.

[52] Franken and Kalsbeek, 1969, Fig. 50:108-109; 51:1,4,16; 54:103,108; 57:33; 60:6; 62:7,10,13; 65:9-10,19; Rast, 1978, Fig. 11:4.

[53] Franken and Kalsbeek, 1969, Fig. 46:73; 51:31-32; Rast, 1978, Fig. 3:2.

[54] Franken and Kalsbeek, 1969, Fig. 50:102; 54:124; McNicoll *et al.*, 1992, Pl. 52:13,17; Rast, 1978, Fig. 11:8,10.

[55] Franken and Kalsbeek, 1969, Fig. 73:3.

[56] Dornemann, 1983, 65,76; Franken and Kalsbeek, 1969, 172-174; Fig. 65:33; 67:54; 70:41; 75:89; Rast, 1978, Fig. 8:14;11:6.

[57] Dornemann, 1983, 65,76; Franken and Kalsbeek, 1969, 172-174; Fig. 51:31-32,63-64; 54:119; 60:2,21,22; 67:54; 67:53-56; 70:37-38; Rast, 1978, Fig. 8:14.

[58] Dornemann, 1983, 71: type 233; Franken and Kalsbeek, 1969, 172-174; Fig. 52:1; 55:11; 57:51; 60:27,30.

[59] Franken and Kalsbeek, 1969, Fig. 51:63-64; 67:54.

[60] Herr and Najjar, 2001, 324-328, Fig. 9.4 top; Herr, *et al.*, 1991, 159, 161, Fig.5:9-10.

[61] Possibly of same jar as Fig.4:20.

[62] Herr, *et al.*, 1991, 161, Fig.5:3,8.

[63] Amiran, 1969, Pl.77:3-6; Herr, *et al.*, 1991, 161, Fig.5:3,8; Rast, 1978, Fig. 4:1.

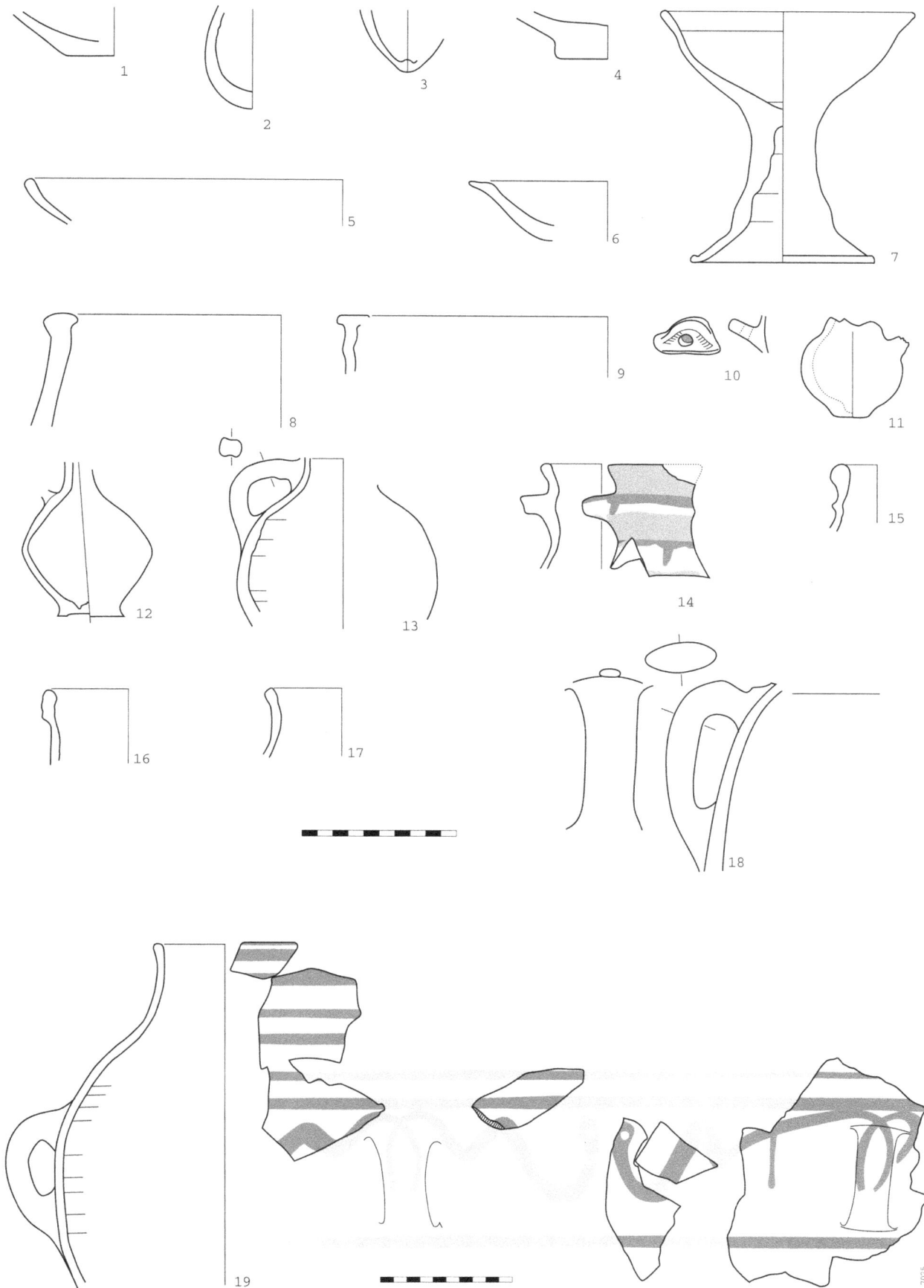

FIG. 4.3: IRON AGE I-IIC POTTERY

[64] Franken and Kalsbeek, 1969, Fig. 53:16; 68:3; McGovern, 1986,Fig.54:52-55,58; Rast, 1978, Fig. 90:2-3; Fischer, 1997, 59-60, Fig. 22:1.

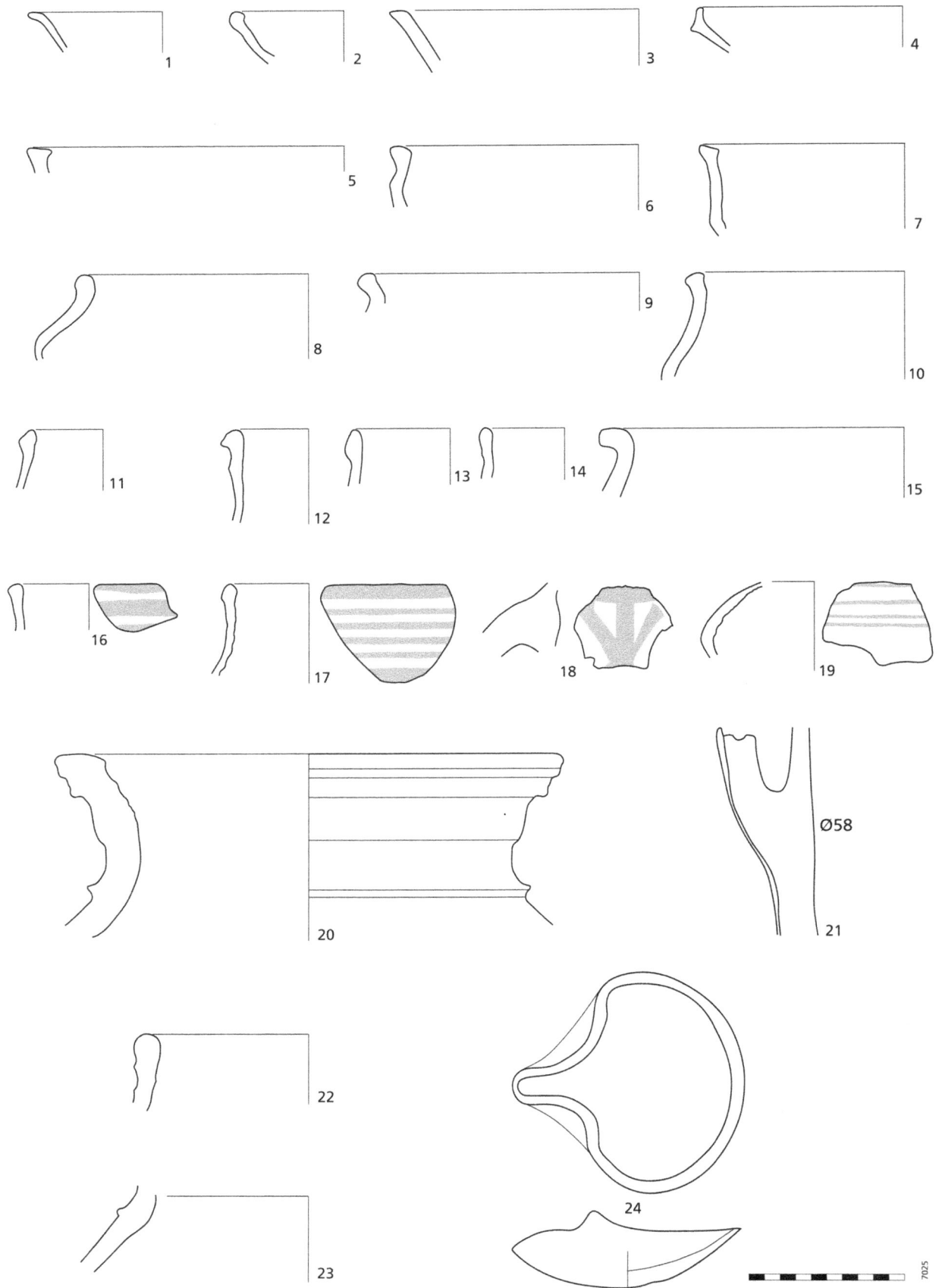

FIG. 4.4: IRON AGE I POTTERY

4.5: Late Bronze II - Iron Age I pottery

Fig.4.5	Description (date)	Phase
4.5:1	Rounded base. Inside finished by adding (a slab of) clay. (LBII-IA I) [65]	IV.5 (P2b)
4.5:2	Flat base. Inside finished by adding (a slab of) clay. (LBII-IA I) [66]	IV.5 (P2a)
4.5:3	Small bowl. (LBII-IA I) [67]	IV.2
4.5:4	Small bowl. (LBII-IA I) [68]	IV.5 (P2a)
4.5:5	Shallow bowl. (LBII-IA I) [69]	IV.4
4.5:6	Shallow bowl. (LBII-IA I) [70]	IV.4
4.5:7	Bowl. (LBII-IA I) [71]	IV.5 (P2b)
4.5:8	Bowl. Slight ochre slipped and burnished on interior. (LBII-IA I) [72]	IV.5 (P2a)
4.5:9	Shallow bowl. (LBII-IA I) [73]	surface/IV.3
4.5:10	Shallow bowl. (LBII-IA I) [74]	IV.5 (P2b)
4.5:11	Pilgrim's flask, body sherds. Concentric bands painted. (LBII-IA I) [75]	IV.4-IV.5 (P2b)
4.5:12	Crater. Ochre slip and bands painted on rim. (LBII-IA I) [76]	IV.5 (P2b)
4.5:13	Crater. (LBII-IA I) [77]	III.1
4.5:14	Crater. (LBII-IA I) [78]	IV.5 (P2b)
4.5:15	Cooking amphora. (IA I) [79]	IV.3

4.6: Late Bronze II - Iron Age I pottery

Fig.4.6	Description (date)	Phase
4.6:1	Jar. (LBII-IA I) [80]	IV.5 (P2a)
4.6:2	Jar. (LBII-IA I) [81]	II.2
4.6:3	Jar. (LBII-IA I) [82]	II.2
4.6:4	Jar. (LBII-IA I) [83]	IV.3
4.6:5	Jar. Base inside finished smearing out extra clay. (LBII-IA I) [84]	IV.2
4.6:6	Jug. (LBII-IA I) [85]	IV.2
4.6:7	Jar. (LBII-IA I) [86]	IV.3
4.6:8	Jar. (LBII-IA I) [87]	IV.5 (P2b)
4.6:9a-d	Jar. Frieze of alternating straight and serpentine lines, monochrome painted on slipped surface (LBII-IA I) [88]	IV.3

[65] Franken and Kalsbeek, 1969, 102-103.

[66] See previous footnote.

[67] Franken, 1992, Fig.7-16:33; McNicoll *et al..*, 1992, Pl. 28:9,13; Franken and Kalsbeek, 1969, Fig. 46:23; 49:83; 54:23-24; 59:50; 61:78,82; 64:46; 66:76; 69:60-62); Rast, 1978, Fig.3:9-12; 5:1; 8:3-5,7,10-11; 13:6.

[68] See previous footnote.

[69] McGovern, 1986, Fig.33:3; McNicoll, *et al,* ,1992, Pl. 2, Fig. 28:6,8; 47:8; Franken and Kalsbeek, 1969, Fig. 46:37,39; 54:45,55; 59:67; 61:71; 71:82-83; 75:34.

[70] Franken, 1992, Fig.7-16:66,72; McNicoll *et al.*, 1992, Pl. 28:9,13; 43:6-9, Franken and Kalsbeek, 1969, Fig. 46:38; 49:56-57; 54:23,45; 59:67; 61:78,82; 64:46; 66:76; 67:5; 69:60-62); Rast, 1978, Fig.3:7-8; 5:1; 8:1-2,6; 13:2-3.

[71] McNicoll *et al.*, 1992, Pl. 35:17;43:15-16; Franken, 1992, Fig.7-16:67-69; McGovern, 1986, Fig.50:14-17; Franken and Kalsbeek, 1969, Fig. 54:38,40;56:70-72;64:48,51.

[72] McNicoll *et al.*, 1982, Pl.122:4; McNicoll *et al.*, 1992, Pl. 35:17-18; 43:16-17; Franken and Kalsbeek, 1969,. Fig.46:42; 54:52.

[73] Franken and Kalsbeek, 1969, 157-159, Fig. 64:105-106; 67:29; 75:52; McNicoll *et al.*, 1982, Pl. 47:11.

[74] See previous footnote.

[75] McGovern, 1986, Fig. 42:12; Franken and Kalsbeek, 1969, Fig. 46:88; 60:31; Briend and Humbert, 1980, Pl. 62:9; 74:4-5; 75:4.

[76] McNicoll *et al.*, 1992, Pl. 49:1,13; Franken, 1992, Fig.7-18:152,156,158,164; McGovern, 1986, Fig.51:25; Franken and Kalsbeek, 1969, Fig. 59:114 (cf. 55,69,74,79,85,97,102); Fischer, 2006, 191, Fig. 228:2.

[77] Franken, 1992, Fig.7-18:149-150; 7-21:38; 7-22:97; McNicoll *et al.*, 1992, Pl. 49:11; 52:6; Franken and Kalsbeek, 1969, Fig. 59:111-113 (cf. 62:23-25); cf. Rast, 1978, Fig. 4:8.

[78] McNicoll *et al.*, 1992, Pl. 48:12,13; McGovern, 1986, Fig. 35:4; Franken and Kalsbeek, 1969, Fig. 46:21.

[79] McNicoll *et al.*, 1992, Pl. 65:8; Tubb, 1988, 42, fig.19:9; Rast, 1978, Fig. 21:5; Gilboa and Sharon, 2003, 28, fig.8:16.

[80] Franken, 1992, Fig.7-19:215-222; 7-21:54,57; Franken and Kalsbeek, 1969, Fig. 57:36-37; 60:22; 62:18; Rast, 1978, Fig. 11:3; 24:3.

[81] Franken, 1992, Fig.7-19:227; 7-21:54,57; Franken and Kalsbeek, 1969, Fig. 50:102; 57:39; Rast, 1978, Fig. 88:2; McNicoll *et al.*, 1992, Pl. 52:17.

[82] Franken, 1992, Fig. 7-21:63; Franken and Kalsbeek, 1969, Fig. 46:73; McGovern, 1986, Fig. 52:36.

[83] Franken, 1992, Fig.7-19:227; McGovern, 1986, Fig. 37:6; Franken and Kalsbeek, 1969, Fig. 46:85; 51:33; McNicoll *et al.*, 1992, Pl. 52:12-13.

[84] Franken, 1992, Fig.7-19:211—212,231; Franken and Kalsbeek, 1969, 102-102; McNicoll *et al.*, 1992, Pl. 65:5,9.

[85] See footnote 81.

[86] See footnote 81.

[87] Franken, 1992, Fig.7-19:212; McNicoll *et al.*, 1992, Pl. 52:16; Franken and Kalsbeek, 1969, Fig. 46:72; 51:24; 57:37; 60:19; 62:18; Rast, 1978, Fig. 6:4; Fischer, 1997, 43, Fig.12:1.

[88] Franken, 1992, Fig.7-4:54; 7-10:60; 7-14:1-2; Franken and Kalsbeek, 1969, 172-174, Fig. 51:56; 52:4; 57:47; 60:29; 65:54; cf. Dornemann, 1983, 67: type 58.

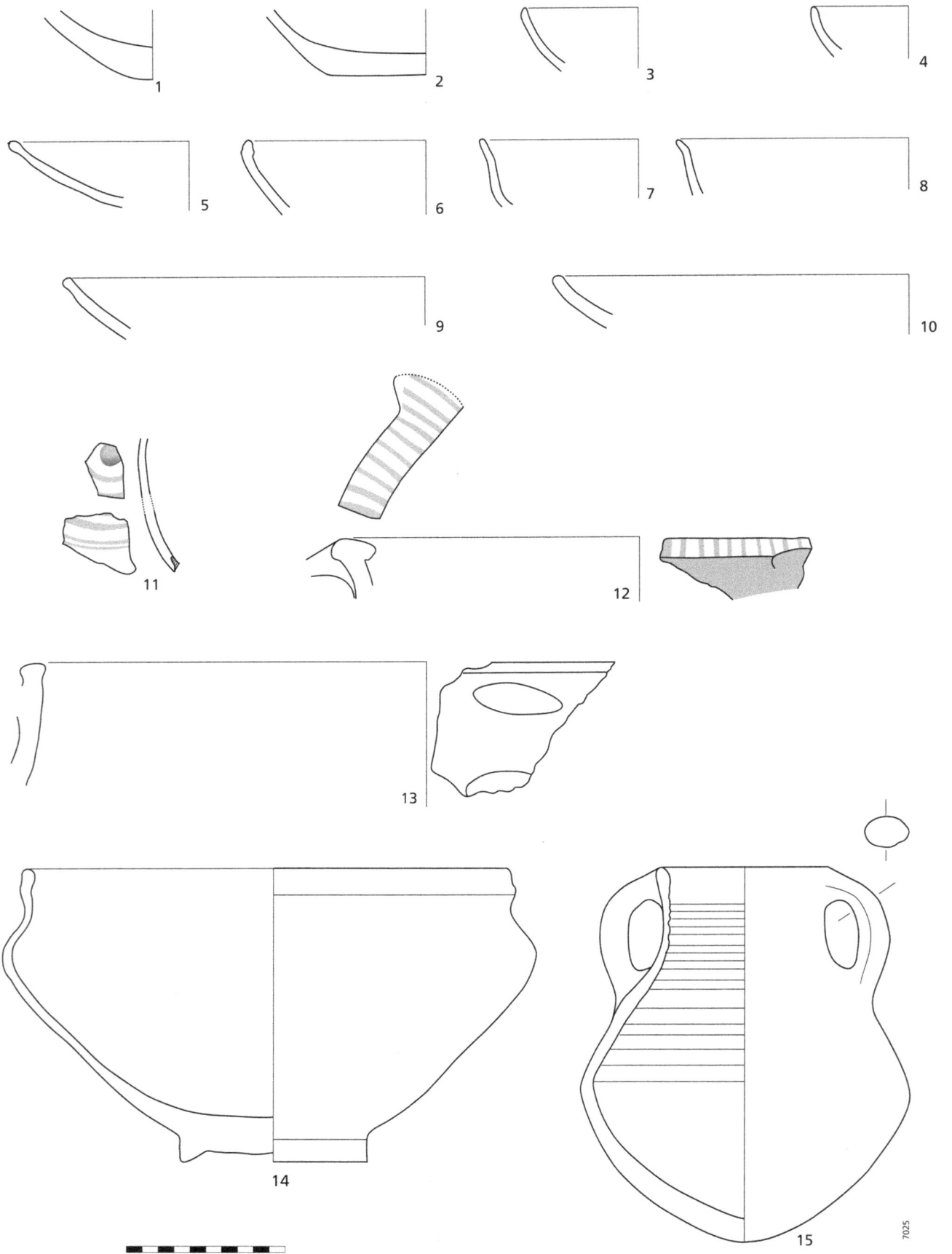

Fig. 4.5: Late Bronze II - Iron Age I pottery

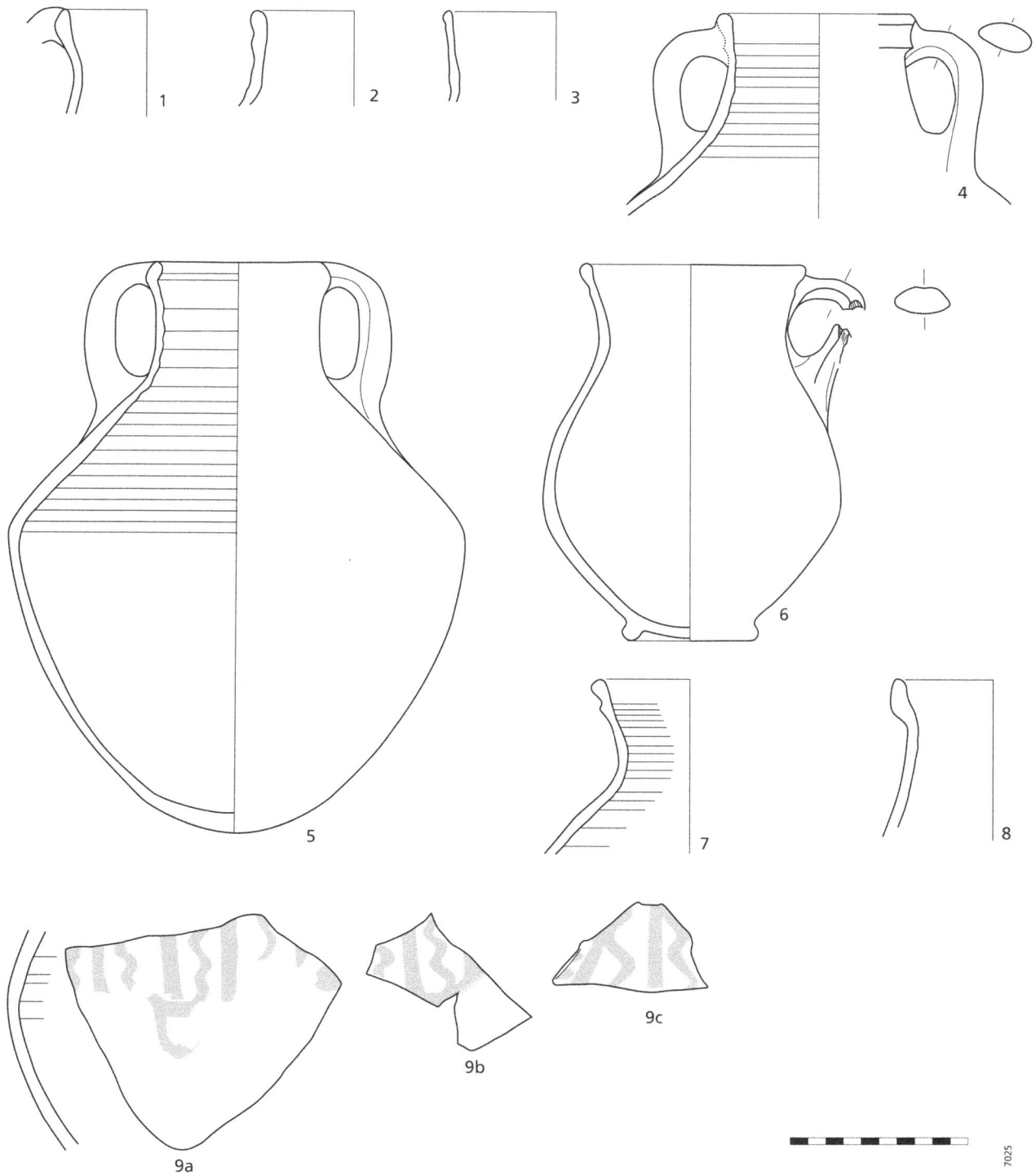

FIG. 4.6: LATE BRONZE II - IRON AGE I POTTERY

4.7: Late Bronze II - Iron Age I-IIA pottery

Fig.4.7	Description (date)	Phase
4.7:1	Cookingpot (IA I) [89]	IV.4
4.7:2	Cookingpot (IA I)	I.3
4.7:3	Cookingpot (IA I)	IV.5 (P2a)
4.7:4	Cookingpot (IA I) [90]	IV.5 (P2a)

[89] Franken and Kalsbeek, 1969, 120-123: type 1, *passim* Figs. 46; 49; 53; 59; 61; 63; McNicoll *et al.*, 1992, Pl. 67:4-5.
[90] Franken and Kalsbeek, 1969, 123-127: type 2A, *passim* Figs. 46; 59; 61; 63; McNicoll *et al.*, 1992, Pl. 51:4.

4.7:5	Cookingpot, sharp carination (LBII-IA I) [91]	IV.4
4.7:6	Cookingpot (IA I) [92]	I.4
4.7:7	Cookingpot (IA I-IIA) [93]	III.1
4.7:8	Cookingpot (LBII-IA I) [94]	IV.5 (P2b)
4.7:9	Cookingpot with flaring rim. (IA I) [95]	IV.2
4.7:10	Cookingpot (LBII-IA I) [96]	II.2
4.7:11	Cookingpot (LBII-IA I) [97]	IV.2

4.8: Middle Bronze IIC – Iron Age I pottery

Fig.4.8	Description (date)	Phase
4.8:1	Shallow bowl/cup, inside light brown bands painted on near white slip. (LBII) [98]	I.4
4.8:2	Thin walled bowl, white slipped. (LBII) [99]	IV.5 (P2a)
4.8:3	Bowl, white slipped. (LB) [100]	V.2
4.8:4	Carinated bowl, white slip, burnished. (MBIIC-LBII) [101]	IV.5 (P2b)
4.8:5	Chalice, ochre slipped. (LBII-IA IA) [102]	IV.5 (P2b)
4.8:6	Bowl. (LB) [103]	IV.5 (P2b)
4.8:7	Crater. (LB) [104]	IV.5 (P2b)
4.8:8	Crater. (LBII) [105]	II.1
4.8:9	Jug. (LBII-IA I) [106]	IV.1
4.8:10	Chalice/bowl?, painted bands inside and on rim. Not slipped. (LBII) [107]	IV.5 (P2a)
4.8:11	Jug. Body sherd, "net"-motive painted on pink slip. (LBII) [108]	III.2
4.8:12	Jug. Body sherd. Bichrome painted bands ([weak] red and dark redd.gray) on pink slip. (LBII) [109]	III.2
4.8:13	Idem.	II.2
4.8:14	Idem.	IV.5 (P2a)
4.8:15	Jug/chalice? Body sherd, bichrome (dusky red and black) painted on pinkish white slip (LBII) [110]	II.2
4.8:16	Jug. Body sherd, vertical and horizontal bands (reddish brown) painted on pinkish white slip. (LBII-IA I) [111]	IV.5 (P2a)
4.8:17	Pilgrim's bottle. Neck, reddish brown bands painted on white slip. (LBII) [112]	IV.5 (P2b)
4.8:18	White Slip II ware, milkbowl, rim with ladder pattern. (LBII) [113]	IV.2
4.8:19	White Slip II ware, milkbowl, body sherd with ladder pattern. (LBII)	IV.2
4.8:20	Cooking pot. (LBII-IA I) [114]	IV.5 (P2a)
4.8:21	Cooking pot. (LBII) [115]	IV.3

[91] Franken and Kalsbeek, 1969, 118-119: type 2 (LB), 123-127 type 2A, Fig. 59:20; Franken, 1992, Fig.7-19/20:245,248-249.

[92] Franken and Kalsbeek, 1969, 123-127: type 2F, Figs. 61:46; 64:4; 69:41; 71:48.

[93] Franken and Kalsbeek, 1969, 123-127: type 2, Figs. 64:5; McNicoll *et al.*, 1992, Pl. 64:2; Rast, 1978, Fig. 69:4.

[94] Franken and Kalsbeek, 1969, Figs. 66:52; 71:53; McNicoll *et al.*, 1992, Pl. 48:12.

[95] Franken and Kalsbeek, 1969, 120-123: type 1, *passim* Figs. 46; 49; 53; 59; 61; 63; McNicoll *et al.*, 1992, Pl. 51:6-8; 65:10; Rast, 1978, Fig. 2:8; 17:12.

[96] Franken, 1992, Fig.7-7:34; McNicoll *et al.*, 1992, Pl. 48:9; 50:15.

[97] Amiran, 1969, Fig. 42:14,16; McGovern, 1986, Fig. 37:6; McNicoll *et al.*, 1982, Pl. 119:16; 120:2; McNicoll *et al.*, 1992, Pl. 45:4; Fischer, 2006, 134, Fig.145:4.

[98] Franken, 1992, Figs.7-4:23-24; 7-7:5.

[99] McGovern, 1986, Fig. 25:3-4; 28:10-11; 30:8-9.

[100] McNicoll *et al.*, 1992, Pl. 54:5; Franken, 1992, Figs.7-1:12-13; 7-5:9-10.

[101] Franken, 1992, Figs.7-1:12-13; 7-5:9-10; 7-12:10-11; McNicoll *et al.*, 1982, Pl. 106:5,7,9; McNicoll *et al.*, 1992, Pl. 54:5; cf. Fischer, 2006, 57, Fig. 42:7.

[102] McGovern, 1986, Fig. 33:*passim*; 50:21; McNicoll *et al.*, 1982, Pl. 119:5; Franken and Kalsbeek, 1969, Figs. 45:31-32; 48:53,61-64; 56:32-33; 58:59; Fischer, 2006, 145, Fig.157:1-6.

[103] Franken, 1992, Figs.7-8:6; McNicoll *et al.*, 1982, Pl. 119:6.

[104] McGovern, 1986, Fig. 22:27; Amiran, 1969, Pl. 41:2.

[105] McNicoll *et al.*, 1992), Pl. 49:2.

[106] Franken, 1992, Fig. 7-19:222,234; Pritchard, 1980, fig. 38:1; McNicoll *et al.*, 1982, Pl. 122:7; Fischer, 1997, 37, Fig. 9:2.

[107] Franken, 1992, Fig.7-3:21,23.

[108] Franken, 1992, Fig.7-14:12,14; 7-18:139.

[109] McGovern, 1986, Figs. 36-38,40,42,48: *passim*; Dornemann, 1983, 22, Figs.49,50:*passim*; Franken, 1992, Fig.7-13:27,32,35,37,38; 7-15:9,11; Fischer, 1997, 42-43, Fig. 11:5-6.

[110] Franken, 1992, Fig.7-13:32,35; Fisher, 1999, fig. 13:1-2.

[111] Franken, 1992, Fig. 7-7:44-53; 7-14:*passim*.

[112] McGovern, 1986, Fig. 42:10-12; Fischer, 1997, 47-48, Fig.15:2.

[113] Åström, 1972, 447-457; Franken, 1992, Fig.7-13:42,44; Fischer, 2006, 153, Fig. 164:1.

[114] Franken, 1992, Fig. 7-7:32; McNicoll *et al.*, 1982, Pl. 119:16; 121:2; McNicoll *et al.*, 1992, Pl. 28:4.

4.8:22	Idem.	IV.3
4.8:23	Carinated bowl, interior and exterior pinkish white slip. (LBI-II) [116]	IV.5 (P2b)
4.8:24	Jar/jug, body sherd. Chocolate-on-White. (MBIIC-LBI) [117]	IV.5 (P2a)
4.8:25	Idem.	IV.5 (P2a)
4.8:26	Idem.	IV.5 (P2b)
4.8:27	Cooking pot, rim. (MBIIC-LBI) [118]	IV.5 (P2a)
4.8:28	Cooking pot, rim. (MBIIC-LBI) [119]	IV.5 (P3)

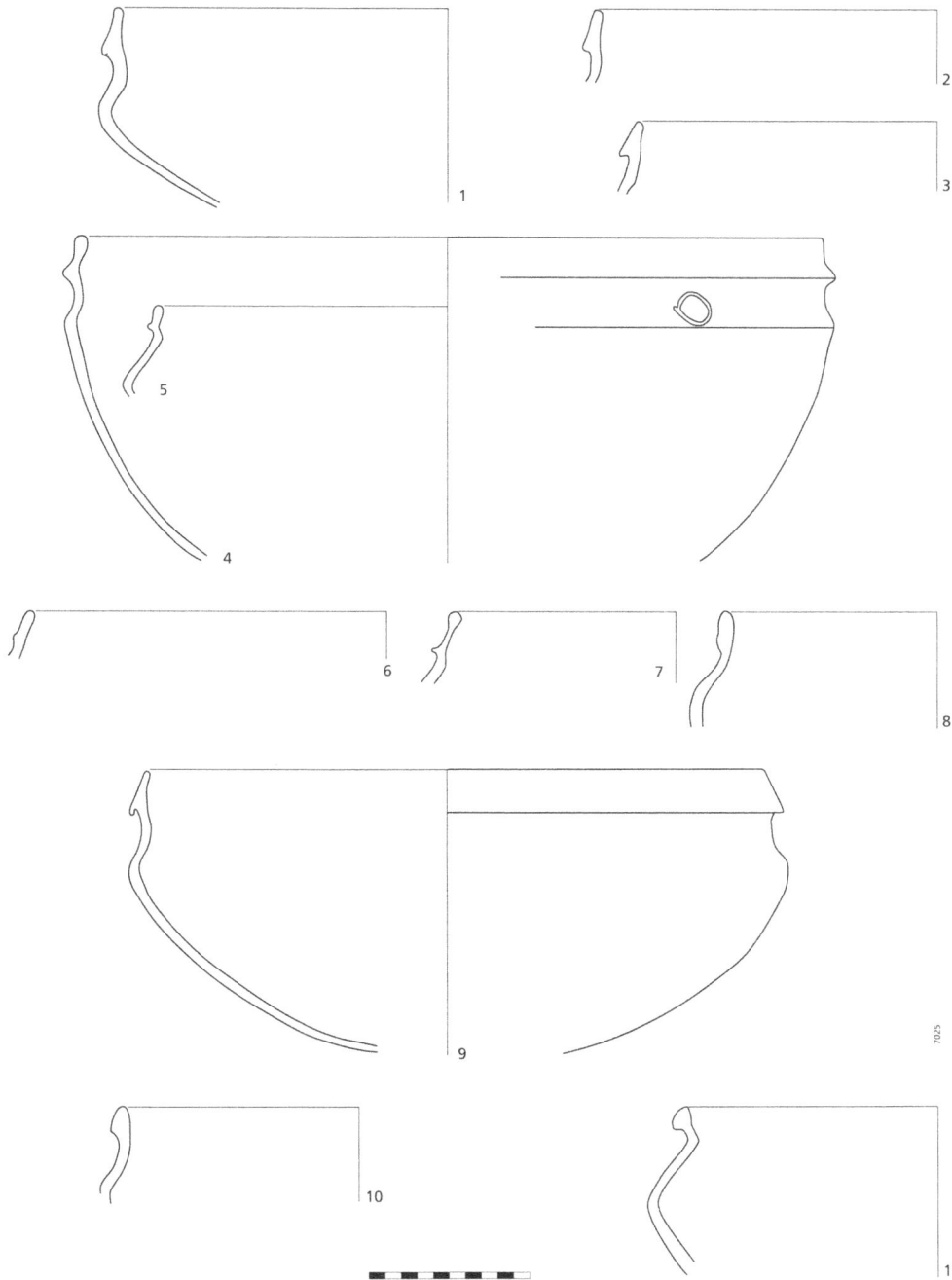

FIG. 4.7: LATE BRONZE II - IRON AGE I-IIA POTTERY

[115] Franken and Kalsbeek, 1969, 118-119 type 2 (LB), 123-127 type 2G; Fig. 64:5; 66:43; 74:38,41; Franken, 1992, Fig. 7-19:239,245; McNicoll *et al.*, 1992, Pl. 65:12.

[116] Amiran, 1969, Fig. 39:1-9,15-16; Franken, 1992, Fig.7-1:12; 7-5:8-10; 7-10:27-29; 7-12:10-11; McGovern, 1986 Fig. 18:2; 25:15,19; Fischer, 1997, 33, Fig. 6:4; Fischer, 2006, 51, Fig. 37:3.

[117] McNicoll *et al.*, 1992, Pl. 56:5; 57:1,4; 58:5; 59:1; 119:16; 120:2; Fisher, 1993, Fig. 10:1-5,7-8; Hennessy, 1985, 100-113.

[118] McNicoll *et al.*, 1992, Pl. 34:21; 45:2-3; Fischer, 2006, 75, Fig.58:6.

[119] McNicoll *et al* , 1992, Pl. 34:22; 45:4-6; Fischer, 2006, 75, Fig.59:2.

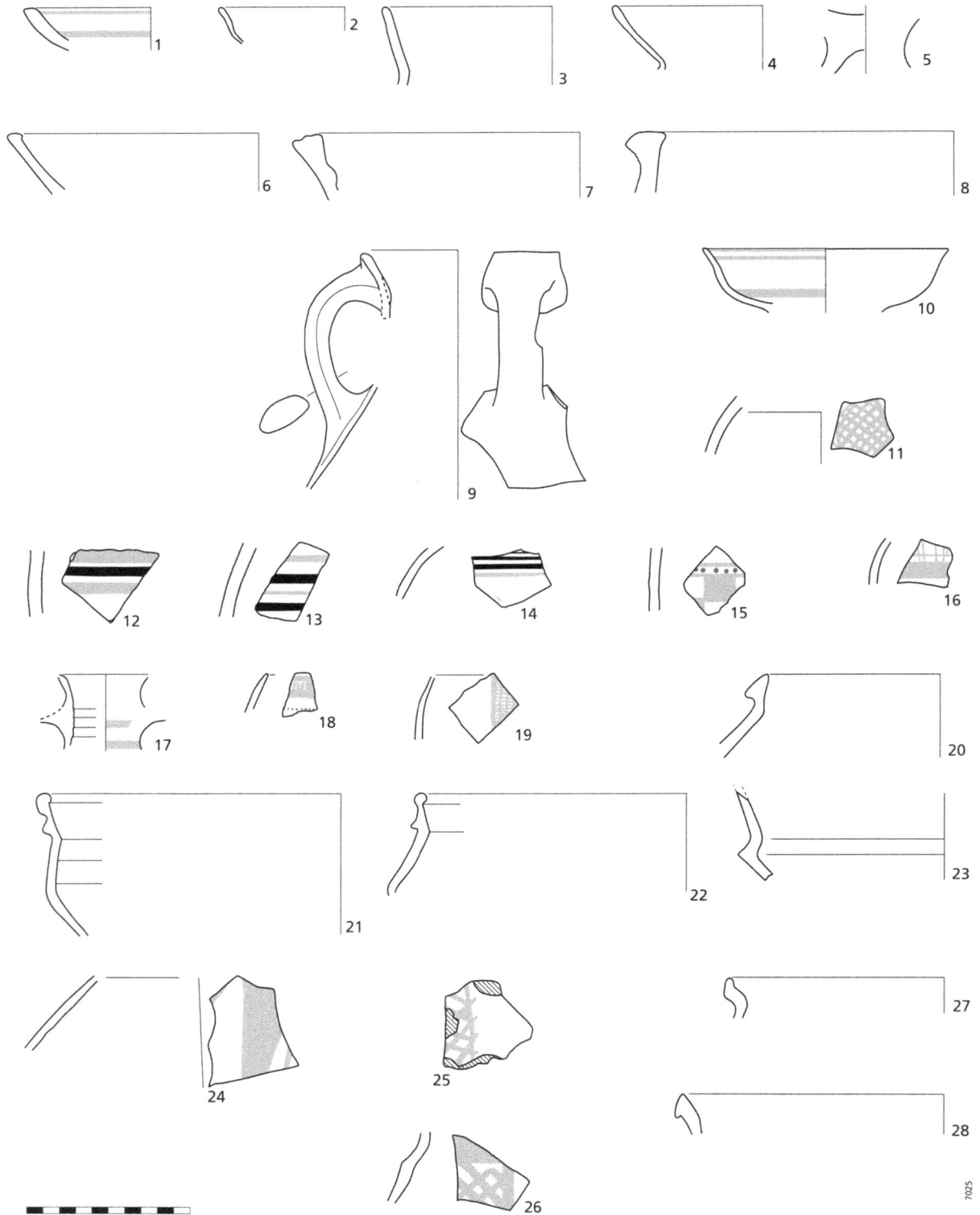

Fig. 4.8: Middle Bronze IIC – Iron Age I pottery

FIG. 4.9: LATE ROMAN - EARLY BYZANTINE COOKING POT (FIG.4.2:1)

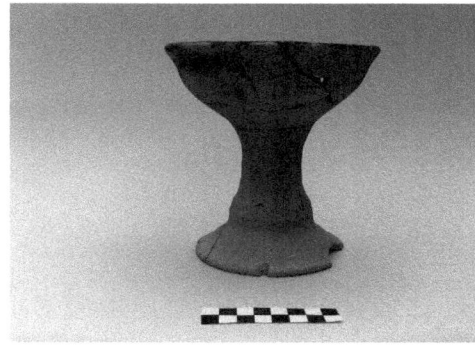

FIG. 4.10: IRON AGE I - IIB CHALICE (FIG. 4.3:7)

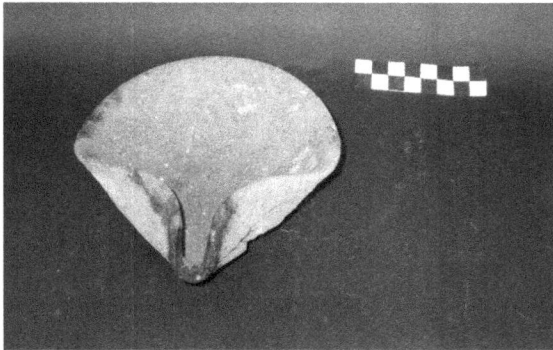

FIG. 4.11: IRON AGE I OIL LAMP (FIG. 4.4:24)

FIG. 4.12: IRON AGE I JAR (FIG. 4.3:19)

FIG. 4:13 LATE BRONZE II - IRON AGE I CRATER (FIG. 4.5:14)

FIG. 4:14 LATE BRONZE II - IRON AGE I JUG (FIG. 4.6:6)

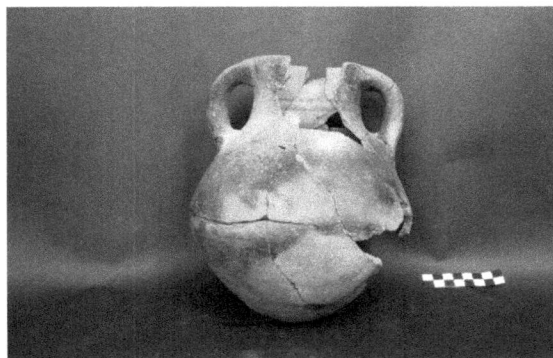

FIG. 4:15 IRON AGE I COOKING AMPHORA (FIG. 4.5:15)

FIG. 4:16 IRON AGE I COOKING POT (FIG. 4.7:9)

EXCURSUS I: PAINTED CERAMICS FROM TALL ZARᶜA[120]

The two campaigns produced a wealth of information about painted ceramics in the Late Bronze and Early Iron Period. Our list of painted ceramics contains about 130 items, in reality somewhat less because a number of fragments were joinable.[121] The range of sherds covers Early Islamic black-and-white (Fig. 4.1:1), glazed pottery (Fig. 4.1:2, 3), Roman-Hellenistic ware,[122] a fragment of black glazed Attic pottery (Fig 4.2,9), but mainly Iron Age and Late Bronze ware, locally made or imported. In Late Bronze context also some Middle Bronze stray finds and perhaps even a single decorated Early Bronze Age sherd. This range tallies with the findings of the initial surveys of Tall Zarᶜa.[123] Here I concentrate on the Late Bronze and Early Iron painted ceramics.

Painted ceramics from the Late Bronze Age
The sondage touched only the top layer of the Late Bronze Age. The majority of the sherds discussed here come from pits and the loamy deposit covering the Late Bronze mudbrick walls and surroundings. Understandably we recovered also a few minor fragments of Middle Bronze IIC sherds, such as white polished 'eggshell' cups and bowls in TZ 1.49 and 2.56 (IV.4–5).[124] Also a rim and carinated shoulder of a small bowl with thin coloured bands on white slib (TZ 2.56+57 [IV.4]), two of them were probably part of a bichrome 'carinated bowl' showing redbrown and black horizontal bands on white slib (TZ 2.38 [IV.1]).

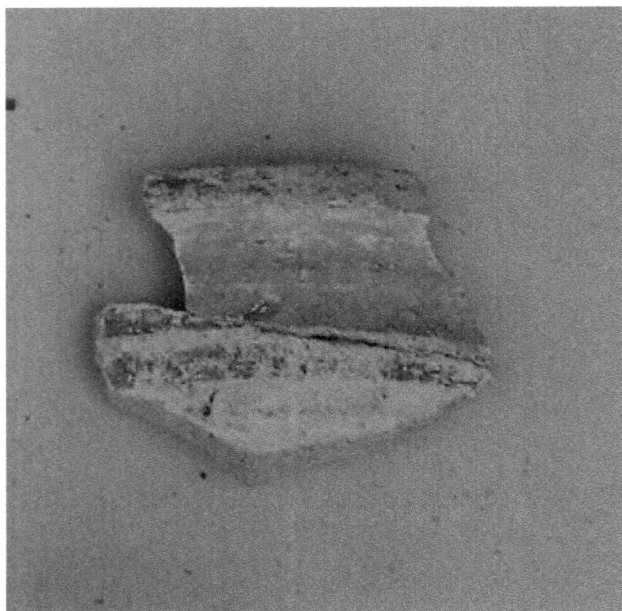

FIG. 4.17 RIM OF MIDDLE BRONZE IIC BOWL TZ 2.56+57.

Chocolate-on-White and similar style
From the Late Bronze Age come some sherds (about 13) with the colours and decoration typical of 'Chocolate-on-White' Ware.[125] Apart from a few items, the fragments were too small to assign them with certainty to a particular kind of pottery. Sherd Fig. 4.8:24 has the fine white slib with 'hanging' triangle decoration often found on the shoulder of Chocolate-on-White jugs.[126] Many of the other sherds are of coarser quality and are seemingly Chocolate-on-White style, but lack the white slip. The geometric decorations (metope, checker pattern (1.24(1)), net pattern (1.61(1); 2.23(2)), framed spirals (2.19); ornamental borders (1.49(3); 1.61(3); 2.52(1)) and stylized trees (1.49(16)[127]; 2.52(2)) made of matte red (sometimes bright) and dark-brown monochrome paint (sometimes almost black) on a white, cream or yellow slip, suggest, in general, Late Bronze (Fig. 4.8.11, 16, 24, 25, 26). According to the typology of Fischer, only a few sherds with slip belong to Chocolate-on-White I–III Ware, that is ceramics of the Late Middle Bronze (Middle Bronze IIC) or, more likely, Early Late Bronze Age (Late Bronze I).[128] Perhaps also a few fragments of bichrome Chocolate-on-White Ware were attested. They could have belonged to a S-bowl with a bichrome band on its shoulder. The fragment with the checker board pattern from locus TZ 1.24 (Fig. 4.8:15) belonged to a chalice.[129]

The quality of the surface differs considerably from thick to very thin slip, or even to self-slip or wash. It is possible that some pieces of pottery were decorated in Chocolate-on-White style (Late Bronze II, Iron Age), but no longer belong to the Chocolate-on-White Ware as such.[130]

'Imported' Cypriote and Mycenean Ware
Two sherds from 'imported' Cypriote 'milk-bowls' (White Slip II) were found (Fig. 4.8:18–19).[131] Though it looks rather similar to Chocolate-on-White Ware, it has a different origin.[132] Clear examples from Mycenean or Aegean Ware were not discovered during our campaigns. There are however two rim fragments with dark-brown (almost black) bands on a caramel polished slip surface from TZ 2.38 and 2.56 (stratum IV.1–4), apparently from

---

[125] TZ 1.24 (1); 1.24 (3); 1.24(4); 1.42; 1.49(3); 1.49(13); 1.49(16); 1.50(2)+1.51(1); 1.61(1); 1.61(3); 2.23(2); 2.52(1); 2.52 (2). About name and typology, see Fischer, 1999, 1–6; idem, 2003, 51–52, Donelly, 2004 , 97–99.
[126] Tell Abu Kharaz, Fischer, 1999, 15 No 3;16 No 2; Salje *et al.* (eds) , 2004, 107 Abb. 5.12 (Pella) etc.
[127] The motif of pendant triangle is most likely an abstraction of the tree-motif, Fischer, 2003, 54 n.11.
[128] Fischer, 1999, 2.
[129] The White Slip and coloured bands were still present though much deteriorated. See Fischer, 1999, 2; Fischer, 2003, 51. For the checker board pattern, see a Middle Bronze / Late Bronze chalice from Lachis; Fischer, 1999, 10 No 2.
[130] On this problem, see Fischer, 1999, 23.
[131] For a recent typology see Beck *et al.*, 2004, 14–15; BAI Wuppertal published a handle in Häser and Vieweger, 2005, 141 Fig. 8 No 11. They were not used to drink milk, but as a kind of serving bowl for hot meals, also as a cup for drinking flavoured wine. Beck *et al.*, 2004, 13. The provenance of these fragments in TZ 2.31 and TZ 2.38 (IV.1) i..e. the deposit on Fl.H and a related floor (Chap. 2) suggest them to be residual.
[132] Fischer, 1999, 4, 20–24, idem, 2003; Donelly, 2004, 97–99.

---

[120] We thank Dr G van der Kooij for his advices on the dating of this material.
[121] References such as TZ 1.49 (16) indicate the Findno. and the number added between brackets the artefact in our list of painted ceramics.
[122] Also some Eastern Terra Sigillata was in evidence (Fig.4. 2, 6-8)
[123] Vieweger, 2002a, b.
[124] Concerning the distinction of this undecorated White Slip (Eggshell) Ware from decorated Chocolate-on-White Ware, Donelly, 2004, 98.

dishes or shallow bowls, which may be Mycenean. Chocolate-on-White ceramics and Cypriote 'milk-bowls' together with Mycenean imports reflect a certain stage of wealth and luxury. They are found in other Late Bronze contexts in the Jordan Valley and in the Uplands (Dayr ᶜAllā, Tall al-Hammah; Tall Abu al-Kharaz, Pella, Tall Ayn Abda, Tall al-Fukhar, Irbid, Amman) and further, for instance Tell Astara in Southern Syria. This evidence at Tall Zarᶜa, now confirmed by the excavations of BAI Wuppertal, suggests that the site of Tall Zarᶜa and the surrounding Wādī al-ᶜArab was not outside the boundaries and routes of international trade. It may even confirm that the site was situated along one of the major trade routes between Palestine and Syria.

Bichrome and Monochrome Ware
A second group of fragments with bichrome decoration usually had a hard-baked and rose or orange surface,[133] which is sometimes polished or provided with a light wash. The term bichrome is not specific, but in this case it means mainly Jordan Valley Bichrome Ware.[134] We assigned about ten sherds to this group. They mainly had a decoration of bands of equal width alternatively dark-blue/black and dark-red. Of interest are a fragment from a small jug (TZ 1.49(14), Pl. 4.8:14) and some rather thick sherds with bichrome bands (TZ 1.23(2); 1.48(3); 2.21(2); 2.23(3), Fig. 4.8:12–13), which were probably part of the same ceramic object. One fragment with a decoration of scales on an orange surface (no slip) (TZ 2.28(3)) is reminiscent of Mycenean Ware (see below)[135] but possibly imitation.

The monochrome group included about twenty fragments.[136] Once more, no complete object was found, but there were pieces that were rather easy and safe to class. First fragments from 'pilgrim bottles' of different size and quality. The neck and some body sherds of a rather large bottle with red-brown en dark-brown painting on a white–yellow surface (not on slip TZ 1.49(5)+, Fig. 4.3:14) and a fragment of a smaller specimen with red bands (on white slip TZ 1.50(3), Fig. 4.8:17). Further some bodysherds (TZ 2.56+1.59, perhaps also 2.49 (2) Fig. 4.4:19; 4.5:11) with red-brown bands on a grey surface (not on slip) and a rim from a crater painted with stripes of oily red slip (TZ 1.61(7), Fig. 4.5:12).

The assortment of painted ceramics from Late Bronze II / Iron Age was quite diverse. There were several specimens of biconical jugs with horizontal and vertical bands, and handles attached to the shoulder (TZ 2.51(2); 2.37+),[137] craters with horizontal handles (TZ 2.39(2); 2.52(3)) and small jugs with red bands on neck and shoulder (TZ 2.26(3); 1.23(2)). Further, there was a

shallow bowl with brown-red bands on the rim and inside (TZ 1.49(12) Pl. 4.8:10), and cups with a painted rim and bands inside (TZ 1.24(6) and 2.8 Fig. 4.8:1). Large parts of an egg-shaped jar were found (TZ 2.30+54; 2.28(1) Fig. 4.6:9a–c). It had orange decoration painted on a polished caramel slip. The decoration around the widest part of the jar consisted of a ring of vertically framed wavy lines. A similar decoration, in this case perhaps painted on the shoulder of the jar is on the left side enclosed by an ornamental border with framed dots, probably alongside the handle. Whereas the bichrome painted ceramics were mainly assigned to the Late Bronze Age, it is probable that the monochrome group continued to be produced in the Early Iron Period.

From about fifty sherds analysed, some were only of interest because of their decorative motives, such as ornamental borders with framed lozenges (TZ 1.30(2)), a net (TZ 2.23(2); 1.49(2) (+) 2.30(2) Fig. 4.8:11, 26); a ladder pattern (TZ 2.38(1) Fig. 4.8:16, 25) and also a faunal motif (TZ 1.24(5) bird?) or floral ornament (TZ 2.52). Like the Middle Bronze fragments, the majority of these Late Bronze 'residual sherds' did not carry much stratigraphical weight because they usually stemmed from refuse pits, fills and foundation trenches. They were, however, evidence of 'imported' and other pottery types from Middle Bronze IIC and Late Bronze I at Tall Zarᶜa. For better examples, we did not reach deep enough into original Late Bronze floors and layers. But Cypriote and Mycenean sherds were in evidence, in particular from Pits P2 and P3 and the loam deposit, in which the pits were dug. Some fragments from this deposit could even be joined to those in the pit and fills.[138] Most painted ceramics assigned by form, material and decoration to Middle and Late Bronze, came from a loam deposit spread over Late Bronze mud-brick walls and large pits and fills under Early Iron Age and Iron Age IIA floors H–K (Stratum IV) and Byzantine floors C–D (Stratum II).

Painted Ceramics from the Iron Age
From about 60 sherds in this group, most were too small or too little diagnostic for proper analysis and assessment. Compared to the Late Bronze Age, decoration became less colourful, less varied and less artistic. In particular, fewer types of motifs were used. There are also no clearly distinctive groups of ware in contrast to the Late Bronze Age. Further, we found no examples of ladder or checker pattern. Floral and faunal motifs became exceptional. Decoration mainly consisted of monochrome red-brown or dark-brown lines in sets of two of three bands, whereas bichrome bands were again the exception and possibly an indication of a later Iron Age II date (TZ 1.48(1)). These band decorations were found on the neck of jugs and jars (TZ 1.48(1); 2.26(1); 2.56(5)), the upper part of the shoulder (TZ 1.48(1); 2.26(2); 2.31(1)) or the body (TZ 2.33+). The majority of this ware seems to be locally produced. Real imports were not in evidence apart from an occasional Iron Age IIB item that could be a Phoenician import or imitation. We found parts of a bowl

---

[133] TZ 1.23(1); 1.44(3); 1.48(2); 1.48(3); 1.49(14); 2.21(2); 2.23(3); 2.2 (3); 2.39 (1); 2.57 (2).
[134] To distinguish it from 'Philistine'Bichrome and 'Phoenician' Bichrome ware.
[135] Compare Salje *et al.* (eds), 2004, 107 Abb. 5.13.
[136] TZ 1.30(2); 1.49(2); 1.49(5)+1.4<9>(10)+1.49(11) +1.50(1); 1.49(12); 1.50(3); 2.23(1); 2.26(3); 2.30(2); 2.30+2.54; 2.38(1); 2.39(1); 2.39(2); 2.43; 2.49(2); 2.51(2); 2.52(3).
[137] It could be Iron Age I, see Amiran, 1970, p.183 Iron Age I.

[138] Apart from the MB fragment 2.56(7)+2.57(1), also the CoW sherd 1.50+1.51; *tannūr* sherds 1.61+1.62 and parts of the jug/jar 2.56+2.57.

with polished orange slip and dark red borders and spirals (TZ 1.43(3)(+)1.44(3)(+)1.46(3)) and a biconical juglet with a polished copper-like surface (TZ 1.49+50; Fig. 4.3:12).[139] The stratigraphic context of these finds suggests, however, Iron Age IIA at the latest. The biconical juglet might also be an Early Iron imitation of a Late Bronze *bilbil*.[140]

Outstanding in this Early Iron painted group was an ovoid jar with handles on the body (TZ 2.15+), a set of bands on the rim and neck, and a frieze with serpent motif, their tails crossed over the handles (Fig. 4.3:19; 4.12). It looks like a simpler 'sister' of the beautiful jar discovered by BAI Wuppertal.[141] Also noteworthy were a few joining body sherds from a biconical jug (TZ 2.33+2.37), the neck and shoulder from some small jugs with bands on both (TZ 1.23(2); 2.26(3)), and the rim and neck with red bands from jars (TZ 2.56(5); 2.57(3); Fig. 4.4:16, 17).

Finally, we observed rims from cups, dishes or (shallow) bowls (TZ 1.49(7); 1.51(2); 1.61(4); 2.8; 2.26(4); 2.56(4); 2.58). The decoration is rather simple. It varies from one single painted band on top of the rim (TZ 1.49(7), 1.51(2)), some bands inside (TZ 2.8), or outside (TZ 1.61(4), also on top of the rim) to bands on both sides (TZ 2.56(4)). On one handle, a cross of red-orange slip was painted (TZ 1.38 Fig. 4.4:18). The colour was usually bright red or dark-red on a cream or orange-washed surface. There were also some fragments with broad red-brown bands on a polished surface of orange slip (TZ 2.23(1), 2.46, 2.55). They apparently came from a quite large container. We also had some Iron Age II fragments of pithoi covered with orange slip.

In conclusion most of the painted ceramics stem from the Early Iron Period and only a few from Iron Age II. No painted items from Iron Age IIC were in evidence, in line with the ceramic evidence in general and with the stratigraphy.

EXCURSUS II. MANUFACTURE AND MEASUREMENTS OF POTTERY HANDLES

Among the diagnostic pieces of pottery, handles occur in a great variety of form, material, manufacture and size. "It is evident that handles are important points of observation ...", said the late Henk Franken about the skill of the potter, the usability and typology.[142] Despite variety, they show characteristic features that often help in determining the types of vessels and utensils they belonged to. We collected all the handles and pottery fragments with vestiges of handles, in particular of how

they were attached to rim, shoulder and body and the manner they broke off from the vessel.[143] Altogether 264 handles and fragments were recorded. From these 264 handles, about 50 were identified as 'milked' of 'pulled' handles from the Iron Age II period (Table 4.1).

In transverse section, the earliest Iron Age handles often had a round, triangular or flattened profile and did not differ much in thickness above and below (e.g. Fig. 4.3:18, 19). At this stage, handles were made from a coil of folded and rolled paste of less plastic clay, of which both extremities were attached perpendicular to the rim, the wall and on the shoulder of the jar, sometimes affixed with a supportive strip of clay. Often the folded and rolled coil of clay was slightly flattened so that the section showed a more oval profile in the middle part of the handle. Another way of attachment was to attach the upper end onto the rim, neck, shoulder or body, pressing the edges of this end on the vessel so that the upper part of the grip became broader, whereas the lower part was modelled into a somewhat thinner end that was obliquely pressed on the body of the vessel often strengthened with a small band of clay whereas superfluous clay after attachment was scraped away or smoothed out with a tool.[144] If such a handle breaks off, it often clearly shows an imprint of the end of the handle, whereas the rim of attachment was left behind. This type of flattened handle and oblique attachment of the lower end was further developed into the 'pulled' handle, usually assigned to Iron Age II. Alongside other techniques of making handles, this technique came into broader use with the much faster production of thrown pottery,[145] but in the transitional stage it was still found with hand-made pottery. Such a handle was made from a lump or cone of plastic clay paste, which was pulled between thumb and index finger by a 'milking' movement, sometimes shaped between thumb and two or three fingers into a handle tapering toward the lower end. It was attached to the vessel in the same way as above. In transverse section the profile was then flat with sharp edges and the surface showed the grooves of the longitudinal 'milking' movements. Only about 19% of the collected handles were of this latter type and they stem mainly from storage jars. This proportion tallies with the scarcity of Iron Age IIB–C material in our sondage.

In our recording, we distinguished two types of storage jars and pithoi according to the place where the handles had been attached, i.e. to the shoulder or to the wall of the body. Jar Type 1 and Pithoi Type 1 had handles almost vertically attached to the wall of the jar under the shoulder, sometimes on the edge between shoulder and body. The attachment of both ends of the handle was sometimes tending towards semi-circular and in section the profile was round or slightly oval (Jar Type 1a, Fig. 4.3:19). However, the handle was more often slightly flattened,

---

[139] Usually called Cypro-Phoenician Ware or 'Black-on-Red'. On this misnomer, see Amiran, 1970, 286ff.

[140] Amiran, 1970, Pl. 84, 92; Yon, 1981, 38; Dayani, 1970, 32 SA 148 (Pl. IV).

[141] Vieweger and Häser, 2007b, 155.

[142] Franken and Kalsbeek, 1969, 170–171; also the special contribution of J. Kalsbeek in Franken and Kalsbeek, 1969, 86–87; Franken, 1974, 78–79 Fig. 2; Franken and Kalsbeek, 1975, 63; Franken, 1993-1994, 47-53; we basically followed Franken's terminology.

[143] Franken and Kalsbeek, 1969, 87.

[144] Franken, 1969, 171.

[145] Franken, 1993-1994, 49.

	Jugs	Jars Type 1	Jars Type 2	Jars indeterm.	Pithoi	Juglets	Kraters	Indeterm.	Total
LB / IA I	30	31	13	33	18	16	8	65	214 ≈ 81 %
IA II	3	7	3	0	4	4	8	21	50 ≈19 %
	33	38	16	33	22	20	16	86	264 = 100%

Table 4.1 Number and proportion of handles assigned to type of vessel.

	d N / S	d	h	$l; h; b$	b at the top	b at the lower end	th at the top	th at the lower end
Pithoi, $N = 4$	27/34	45	-	150; 64; 29	5,1	4,0	2,3	2,0
All pithoi	28	>39	?	128; 60; 24	5,0	4,3	2,6	2,1
Jars, $N = 4$	10	25	45		4,3	3,2	2,0	1,9
All jars	10	35<	45		4,2	3,3	2,2	1,8
Ovoid jugs, $N = 3$	N11/S 19	26	35	100; 54; 34	3,8	3,1	1,8	2,0
Jug with footstand	N 12.5	17	21.5	90; 40; 25	3,5	3,0	1,5	2,5
Cooking jugs	N 10/S19	20.5	24		4,0	3,3	2,1	1,9
All jugs	N 7-12 S 16-20	26	35	89 ; >41 ; 25	3,9	3,2	1,8	1,9
Juglets	N 4.7	B 9/11			2,4	2,3	1,3	1,4

Table 4.2 Average size of handles from pithoi, jars, jugs and juglets. b, breadth; l, length of curvature of handle; d, diameter of vessel; h, height of vessel, handle; th, thickness; N= neck, S = shoulder, B = body of the jar; N, number of artefacts. The last four columns give the breadth and thickness of the handle measured at the top and at the lower end of the handle. All values are in centimetres.

the upper end attached perpendicular to the wall,[146] whereas the lower end was attached obliquely and often strengthened with a strip of clay (Jar Type 1b, Fig. 4.3:18). Jar Type 2 and Pithoi Type 2 had the handle attached on the shoulder. Also in Jar Type 2b, the upper end of the handle was fixed perpendicular to the shoulder and the lower end perpendicular or oblique at or near the edge of the shoulder. In about 10 finds of Group 2b, the handle was 'pulled' and so was assigned to Iron Age II.

Comments on the results (Tables 4.1 and 4. 2)
1. The measurement of the few fairly complete handles ($N = 4$) present a trustworthy standard to allocate most of the less well preserved handles (all pithoi/jars). For instance, the handles of pithoi are about 25% larger than those of jars.
2. The ovoid jars (handles on the body) and jugs (handle on the neck) do not differ much in average size. Usually, the ovoid jar is slightly larger and higher. Interestingly the greater difference is found in the form of the handles.

Affixed to the rim of the jug, the handle of the jug narrows less towards the shoulder and even thickens sometimes somewhat at the shoulder (Fig. 4.5:15; 4.6:4–6). The average thickness measured at the lower end of the handle is therefore slightly higher (Table 4.2, last column). When affixed on the same level of the rim, the handle often bulges a bit above this level (Fig 4.6:1).
3. Point 2 applies also to the smaller jugs with a standing foot and the juglets, which usually have their handle on neck and shoulder.

Large jars or pithoi as distinct from small jars and jugs
Study of the jar handles made clear that some belonged to a kind of storage jar that was much larger than the usual jars and jugs described above. During our sondage, we found also large fragments of the neck, shoulder and body of a pithos with a high neck and a preserved diameter of 58 cm. Similar pithoi have been found elsewhere in Jordan (Tall al-ᶜUmayri),[147] Galilee[148] and

---

[146] Occasionally, it causes the wall to bulge inside the vessel (zie 1/38 Fig. 4.4:18, 2/26)

[147] Herr *et al.*, 2001; Finkelstein, 1996, 204.
[148] See for this 'Galilean' type of pithos different from the usual collared-rim jar, Bloch Smith and Nakhai, 1999, 62–92, 101*ff.*, Fig p.

Southern Syria (Golan). The excavations of BAI Wuppertal at Tall Zarʿa found and restored a complete example.[149] They differ from collared-rim jars in their high neck, though some of them show the diagnostic ridge between neck and shoulder (Fig. 4.4:20, 23) and have instead an elaborated ridged neck (Fig. 4.4:20).[150] This pithos TZ 2.50+51 (Fig. 4.4:20, 21) had its two partly preserved handles below the shoulder on the body. Its occurrence is significant, because the usual type of collared-rim jar was also used in Jordan and was even produced as far south as Wādī al-Mujib (al-Baluʿa) and as late as the 8th Century BCE.[151] Such large pithoi are often also recognizable by the impression of ropes that held them together in the process of production.[152] The evidence from Tall Zarʿa appears to confirm also for the northern region of Transjordan the expectation of Ibrahim and Worschech that the Transjordanian Late Bronze and Early Iron Age culture developed its own catalogue of types of collared-rim jars and related types of pithoi and that its use was not limited to the villages of a 'hill country' population engaged in horticulture.

Findno.	d N	d S/B	Type	Fig.
1/B surface	21		Rim of CRJ	4.4:22
1/17		22 + ridge	Shoulder CRJ	4.4:23
1/49		40	Shoulder CRJ	
1/61			Shoulder CRJ	
2/50+2/51	28	Next to handle d ca 58	CRJ high neck	4.4:20–21
2/56	30		Rim of CRJ?	

Table 4.3 Collared-rim jars (CRJ) and similar large jars.

80, 121; Yadin, 1961, 103; Finkelstein, 1988, 76–77, Fig. 19–20, 109, 275ff; Mazar 1992, 258, Fig. 7.13; 347-348, Fig 8.25; for Jordan, see Steen, 1996, 55ff; Ibrahim, 1978, 116-126; Worschech, 1992, 149–153. This northern type was found in: Hazor, Dan, Horvat Avot, Tel Keisan, Tel Harashim (Khirbet et-Talil 1814 2626 = Tuleil) and Sasa.

[149] Kindly shown to us at the Biblical Archaeological Institute in Wuppertal, 10 June 2008.

[150] They should be distinguished from the 'Galilean' or 'Tyrian' pithoi (see note 148) with high necks, a broad ridge between neck and shoulder and with the handles on the shoulder. They are often smaller than collared-rim jars (Mazar, 1992, 347, Fig. 8.25; Ibrahim, 1978, Plate XIX).

[151] Ibrahim, 1978, 116–126; Gitin, 1990, 120-121; Worschech, 1992, 149–153; Herr et al., 1991, Fig 5–6 etc; Ji, 1995 122–140, esp. 136–137; Finkelstein, 1996, 204; Herr, 2001. The suggestion of Ji that the CRJ disappeared at the end of Iron Age I in Transjordan is contradicted by the evidence from al-Baluʿa.

[152] Franken and Kalsbeek, 1969, 80. We collected a great number of sherds showing these rope impressions (e.g. 1/10(5); 1/16(1); 1/26(3); 1/37+1/42; 1/50(1)+1/51(1); 1/50(3); 1/62 two pieces; 2/18; 2/33; 2/37 two pieces; 2/49) and they are clearly present on the large pithos 2/50+2/51. As may be expected, many of these sherds are rather thick (ca 20–10 mm).

Findnumber	*d* N-S-B / Thickness wall W	*l* of handle attachement	Measures of handles	Types and comments
1/B surface!	N21			Rim CRJ
1/B(1)	42above / W10-13	Above	*b*48/- *th*34/-	Handle
1/7 (2)	42under / W9-14	Under	Not preserved	Handle
1/7 (4)	Not preserved		*b*41/39-*th*38/21	Handle
1/7(6)	>44 / W8-9	under	*b*-/45 -/-	Handle
1/12+1/14				Large fragment base of pithos
1/12(6)	>44 / 10-12	under	*b*-/53 -/-	Handle
1/16 (2)	>44 above / W10-12		*h*? *b*25 *b*65/41 *th*29/20	Handle
1/16 (6)			*b*-/46 *th*-/17	Handle orange slib?
1/17	S22 W20			Shld. with ridge
1/24(1)	32above-36under/ W7-8	*l* 120 both ends on body	*h*61- *b*23 *b*52/37-*th*21/18	Handle
1/25				Base pithos
1/25	N*d*19; W10-15			Rim with rope impr.
1/37+42	32			Large piece of wall holemouth jar?
1/39(1)	38under /W10-11	under	*b*-/ca50	Handle
1/42 (1)			*b*43/42-*th*22/21	Handle
1/43 (5)	40above/ W10-11	under	*b*-/38 *th*-/21	Handle
1/44+45				Base pithos
1/48				Base pithos
1/48	N*d*19			Rim holemouth?
1/48(6)	45above-43/under / W 11-15	*l* 150 on shoulder or higher on body?	*h*64 - *b*23 *b*46/24 *th*32/20	Scraping of body
1/49	S40 W15/20			Shld. with ridge
1/50				Base pithos
1/50 (2)	26above-32under /W 7-9	*l* 115 under edge on body	*h*54 *b*29 *b*52/43-*th*26/23	Handle; yellow wash or slib?
1/50 (7)	>44 under/ W14-16	under	*b*-/48 *th*-/29	Handle
1/51(3)	>44 under/ W8-10	under	*b*-/40 -/16	Scraping of body
1/59 (4)+ 2/50 (14)?	40above /W10-12	above	*b*49/38-*th*19/21	Scraping of body
1/61	*d*? /W15/20			Shld. with ridge
2/3	N*d*18 W10			Rim pithos
2/6	>36 under/ W11-14	under	*b*-/39 *th* -/22	red slib
2/11 (1)	28above-34under/ W 9-11	*l* 125 on wall of body	*h*61 – *b*23/ *b*55/47-*th*22/21	Imprint finger?
2/11(2)	26under? / W 10-11	under	*b*-/43 *th*-/?	Handle
2/28 (3)	37under / W10-11	under	B-/43-D-/25	Handle
2/28				Base pithos
2/30	N*d*36 W12			Rim holemouth?
2/48				Base pithos
2/50+51	*d*52under W10-20	under on wall of body	N? – B >23 B-/50 D-/23	Rope impression
2/56	N*d*30	.		Rim CRJ
Tot Fld 1+2: 39				

Table 4.4 Handles, rims, necks and bases ascribed to CRJ-jars and other large jars and pithoi

5.1 Seal impression on a jar-handle

TZ 1.24; Stratum II.2 found in a fill under a Roman–Byzantine loam floor, deposited over a large pit containing ceramics from the Late Bronze Age and Early Iron Age.

Description: the seal impression is deeply impressed parallel to the edges of the upper part of an Early Iron jar-handle, pinkish white (Munsell 5YR 8/2). A small chip on the outside of the oval groove is missing. The groove is V-shaped. The picture of an quadruped long-horned animal is cut within the oval ring. The animal looks somewhat hump-backed on the left side and has its tail turned upwards. Above the back, there is an object almost round on the right side, but pointed on the left. Oval ring, size 15 mm × 21 mm (Fig. 5.1; 5.5:2).

The seal depicts a single caprine animal despite its symmetrical design. It carries a symbol above its back, be it a sun disk or another astral symbol. Keel *et al.* interpreted animal images and accompanying symbols in the Iron Age as references for particular deities, in this case a female deity, perhaps Anat-Astarte. The use of the seal suggests the existence of a temple nearby and use in an administrative system.[1]

FIG. 5.1 SEAL IMPRESSION ON A JAR-HANDLE TZ 1.24

---

[1] Dijkstra 2009 forthcoming.

5.2 Potter's marks

The circular sign inscribed before firing on a large cooking pot from TZ 1.50+2.54; Stratum IV, 3/5 (Fig. 4.7:4; 5.2) is similar to a Late Bronze / Early Iron letter *ᶜayin*;

FIG. 5.2 COOKING POT WITH POTTER'S MARK TZ 1.50+2.54

On the jar handle from TZ 2.19+2.12; stratum II.1/III.1 the circular imprint is probably made by a reed before firing; the handle from TZ 2.52; stratum IV.3 shows a cross-sign on a jar handle incised after firing (Fig. 5.5:3); similar signs are often found on pottery handles. It may be assumed that signs made before or after firing had a different function. Only marks made before firing could be considered to be potter's marks in the true sense. This applies also to deep imprints made by a thumb or another finger before firing such as those from jar handle TZ 2.11 stratum III.1 (Fig. 4.3:18). They are found in Early Iron IA/B - IIA (Stratum IV) and IA IIB (stratum III) context.

5.3 Bronze arrow head

TZ 2.38.1 = 2.48 Stratum V.2 in yellow loamy soil around large Pit P3, late Late Bronze or Early Iron Age.

FIG. 5.3 BRONZE ARROW HEAD TZ 2.38.1

Description: a complete bronze arrow head in reasonable state of preservation, some corrosion at the surface; leaf-shaped blade with mid-rib and a knob between blade and quadrilateral tang. Length and width 18,5 mm × 92 mm, thickness of the mid-rib: 6 mm, tang 23 mm × 2 mm (Fig. 5.5:1; 5.3).

Late Bronze and Early Iron Age arrowheads are usually of two types.[2] One is shaped like an olive-leaf with a tang fastened inside a reed-shaft, the other is triangular or is shaped like a harpoon with a socket, in which the shaft is laid and fastened. The tang is often quite long in order to lower the lateral pressure in the shaft. This arrowhead displays a squared tang which thickens to form a projecting shoulder at the transition of the blade. This helped to secure its fastening by a piece of string or tendon wound around the shaft, the knob and the stem. The short triangular form was probably intended to penetrate a coat of mail, whereas the narrow, elongated and often leaf-shaped arrowhead was meant to cut easily through cloth, hide and flesh. The oldest bronze arrows were cast in a mould and hardly dressed, or were even left undressed. Later they were hammered into a curved form with sharp edges and they received a fairly prominent rib in the middle, as is also in this arrow head TZ 2.38.1.[3] This type is mostly assigned to the 12th - 11th Century BCE, but it could also be late Late Bronze Age.[4] A typologically late Late Bronze or Early Iron date complies with the provenance of the arrow head. This type of arrow head was also used for inscribed arrow heads.

5.4 A turquoise bead

TZ 2.56 or 2.57; Stratum IV.4, under Floor Fl.K either below in the large Pit P3 or the yellowish loamy soil around it. Late Bronze Age.

Description: biconical bead of a dark blue-green turquoise, slightly damaged on the thinner side; perforated along the length of the bead. Size *h* 12.5 mm; *b* 6.5 mm; diam. of perforation 1mm (Fig. 5.4; 5.5:6). Turquoise in the Levant was mostly mined in Sinai and distributed via Egypt. The type of bead is also Egyptian.[5]

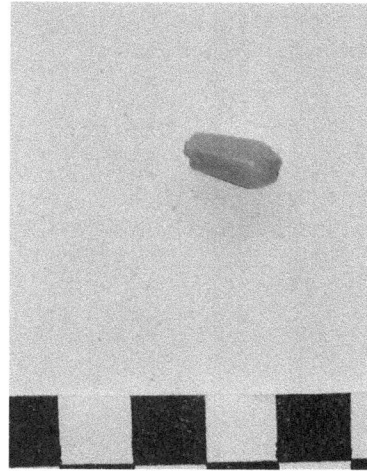

FIG. 5.4 EGYPTIAN TURQUOISE BEAD

5.5 Miscellenea

The first object from TZ 2.56; stratum IV.4 (Fig 5.5:4) a sherd of hard-baked red polished ceramic, which was ground on three sides into trapezoid form. Perhaps, it was part of a pottery tool to scrape away surplus clay.[6] The other object from TZ 2.15; stratum III.1 (Fig. 5.5:5) looks like a ceramic bull's horn and could have been part of a bull figurine or a bovine-form vessel,[7] though it might even be from a sculptured pottery head of a deity (Horvat Qitmit).[8]

5.6 Roman glass handle

The ribbed handle from TZ 1.15 Stratum I.4 (Fig. 4.2:10), is of a well known type belonging to a Roman glass dish/bowl with a diameter of about 22 cm.[9]

---

[2] On the development and manufacture of bronze arrows in relationship to the composite bow in the Late Bronze Age, see Weippert, *BRL²*, 249; Yadin, 1963, 7-8; Gonen, 1975; Mazar, 1992, 265; Philip, 1989.

[3] For such leaf-shaped arrows with a quadrilateral tang, a knob between the leaf and the tang, a mid-rib and a protruding point, see Weippert, *BRL²*, Abb. 64:3 and references.

[4] Beit Arieh, 1985, Fig. 13:10, VIII:17; Seger, 'The Bronzes,' in: Seger and Lance, 1988, 103–104; Pl. 28; for instance, from the 35 arrows in Cave 1.10A, 30 were leaf-shaped; length 80–126 mm, width 13–24 mm.

[5] Wilkinson, 1971; Aldred, 1978.

[6] van der Kooij and Ibrahim, 1989, 93 no. 18; Steel and McCarthy, 2008, 29, Fig. 19.

[7] Steel and McCarthy, 2008, 29, Fig.20; bull figurines Holland, 1977, 126f..

[8] Mazar, 1992, 499, Fig 11.23.

[9] Chapter 2, footnote 21.

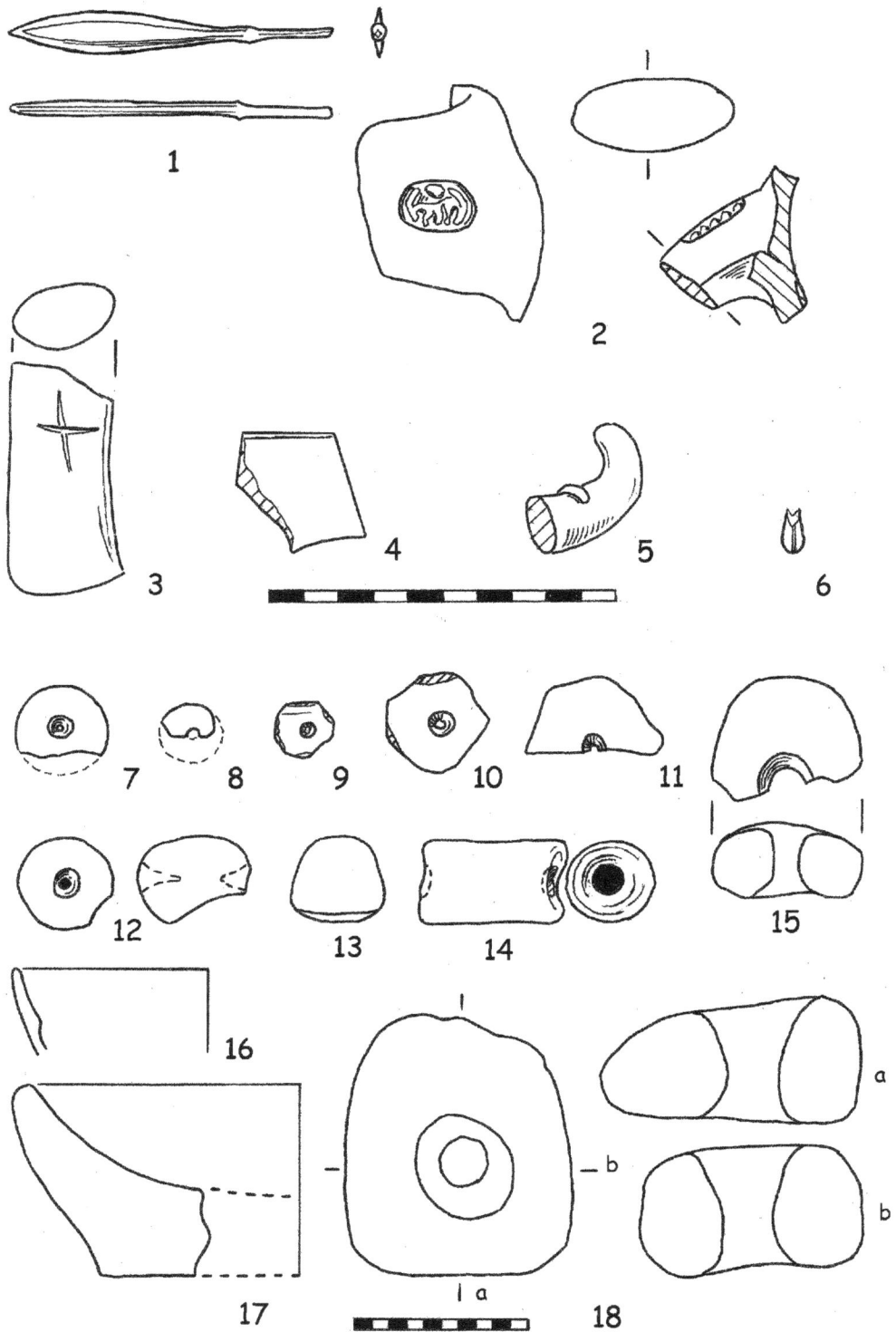

FIG. 5.5: SMALL FINDS AND STONE IMPLEMENTS

6.1 Introduction

About 30 stone implements of different size (Table 6.2), manufacture, use and material and in various states of preservation were discovered, not counting with them about thirty 'sling stones', which we collected as a distinct category. The majority of the utensils are basalt millstones, followed by two or three mortars and a handful of pestles. With a few exceptions they were made of basalt of vesicular, semi-vesicular and compacted quality. The grinding stones (quern or upper stone, also called 'rider'stone) are usually of compacted black basalt, whereas the horizontal lower stones usually have a slightly concave surface and are made of basalt of lesser quality. No objects of sandstone were found and only a few items were of limestone and flintstone.[1] The ratio between basalt and other material is remarkable when compared, for instance, with the situation in Tall Dayr ᶜAllā where 45,5% of all stone utensils were made of basalt and andesite and 44% sandstone and in Middle Bronze / Late Bronze Beth-Shean 78% basalt and 22% limestone or other kinds of stone. The proximity of the Golan and Hauran as a source for basalt may suffice to explain the high proportion of basalt.

	Basalt	Limestone	other	total
Bowls	1			1
Hammer stones	5		2	7
Pestles	2			2
Mortars	2			2
Millstones	12			12
Rings	2		1	3
Rolling pins	1	1		2
Varia	1		1	2
Total number	26	1	4	31
Proportion	84%	3%	13%	100%

Table 6.1 Numbers and proportion of stone objects from different materials.

6.2 Millstones[2]

Only a few of the millstones were found *in situ*,[3] that is close to a clearly defined floor in the proximity of a *tannūr* and/or a cooking place (Fig. 2.14; 2.34). They help to define the excavated area as a domestic setting centred around food preparation (Table 3.1). Many millstones were found broken and reused in walls and other architectural structures. Different types of hand-mills or saddle-querns are represented.[4] Three of the lower millstones belong to the horizontal slightly concave type (Petit Type B1). The broken millstone from TZ 1.29 belonged perhaps to Type Petit B2.[5] The upper millstones are represented by small almost round stones moved by one hand and the long oval stones or (saddle-)querns moved with two hands (Petit Types A1 and A2). The smaller ones are sometimes difficult to distinguish from hammer stones. When flattened at the bottom, we took them for millstones. Some were almost new or little used, others completely worn and broken. A fragment of a large millstone with ribbed surface (TZ 2.29, Stratum II.1 reused in lower stones from Wall W7, Fig. 2.8) was also in evidence (Fig. 6:1), perhaps from the Hellenistic–Roman period.[6]

FIG. 6.1 FRAGMENT OF HELLENISTIC-ROMAN MILLSTONE TZ 2.29

6.3 Pestles and mortars[7]

Different types of mortars were found, all made of basalt. A large bowl-like mortar of irregular form and of rather coarse-grained grey basalt was found complete in TZ 1.59 (Fig. 6.2). Inside was a small trapezoid pestle (Fig. 5.5:13). This large type of basalt bowl is sometimes found *in situ* sunk into the floor like lower millstones.[8] Fragments of a large black basalt mortar (TZ 2.45 (+) 2.49, at the rim diam. 32 mm, at the bottom diam. 22 mm) were found in accumulation of stone (continuation

---

[1] Not counting the flints. Some of the sling stones were made of flint and had served another purpose, for instance as grinding stone in a grinding bowl or something similar.
[2] Kellermann, *BRL²*, 232–233; Amiran, 1956, 46–49; Moritz, 1958; Petit, 1999, 145-167; King and Stager, 2001, 94–95; 152–158; Ebeling and Rowan, 2004, 108–117; Yahalom-Mack, 2007, 639–660.
[3] On top of Wall 6 in the North Section of Field 2, there was a structure made from two lower millstones set upright in an angular position supporting a horizontal stone, perhaps, as a kind of socket for a pillar (in Fig 2.29-2.31 the horizontal stone and the large standing millstone at the back, are still visible, the other millstone was removed).

[4] The term loaf-shaped for the lower millstone does not seem adequate (*pace* Yaholan-Mack, 2007, 651), since this descriptive word applies also to many of the the upper stones.
[5] Though three fragments were recovered, it was still uncomplete.
[6] A complete example is shown in Berlin, 1997, 32.
[7] Dalman, 1933 III, 212-219; Kellermann, *BRL²*, 233; Negev and Gibson, 2003, 209–210; Dajani, 1970, Pl. XVI SA 233; SA 29, SA 136; Ibrahim, 1976, Pls XXIX-XXX.
[8] See Hardin, 2004, 79.

Wall 16?, Pit P3), suggesting a date in the Early Iron Age. It is a large bowl with a disk-like foot well finished outside,

FIG. 6.2 BASALT MORTAR WITH PESTLE TZ 1.59

whereas it is polished inside (Fig. 5.5:17). As in Palestine (Beth Shean, Gezer, Tell Keisan, Tell el-Far‘ah North etc.) basalt mortars in Jordan take many different shapes such as tripod bowls (Dayr ͨAlla, Pella, Sahab, Jabal al-Qusur [Amman], Tall al-Saͨidiyya etc.), rimmed platters, shallow bowls, blocks with a slightly concave depression and so on. This wide basalt bowl seems to be rather exceptional.[9] It was probably imported from Syria. Both small and large pestles are in evidence. It is possible that also 'sling stones' were used as simple grinders, in particular those made of flint. They were perhaps used in ceramic grinding bowls. About ten pottery bowls, some of them on a rather high circular foot, showed an abraded surface inside the bottom. They were probably used as bowls for grinding green herbs and dried leaves (TZ 1.9; 1.25 (2); 1.48 [Fig. 4.3:4]; 1.54; 2.23 (2); 2.31; 2.39 and 2.57). They were all found in Iron Age strata and the majority were associated with floors, herds and other cooking utensils (Table 3:1). Two fragments belonged perhaps to a kind of ceramic mortar known to be an Iron Age imitation of basalt tripod mortars (TZ 2.37; 2.56).[10]

6.4 Weights, spindlewhorls

Implements for spinning and weaving were scarcely represented in the sondage. Only two basalt rings could be provisionally identified as loom or weaving weights from TZ 1.46 (Fig. 5.5:12); 1.49 (Fig 5.5:18); 2.52 (Fig 5.5:15).[11] The first was not completely perforated.[12] It could also be a rolling pin. Because its form is ovoid, it was probably not used for smoothing a large surface such as plaster on the walls of houses, but perhaps for baking or for finishing pottery. Loom weights made of clay and

limestone, elsewhere ubiquitous, were conspiciously absent. The few basalt rings hardly proved the presence of weaving installations and may have served as weights for other purposes. Also the six spindlewhorls from TZ 1.26 (Fig 5.9); 1.49 (Fig 5.10); 1.51 (Fig 5.7);[13] 1.54 (Fig. 5.8); 1.61 (Fig. 5.11); 2.51[14], the majority made of a trimmed ceramic sherd, hardly imply that spinning was a major activity here.

Basalt and limestone stone rings are often found in MB, LB and Iron Age context.[15] Some think that they were used as large weights for domestic purposes and in trade. A similar kind of basalt stone from Tell Bazi (Aleppo Museum M 11127) was suggested to be part of a small grinding mill.[16]

FIG 6.3 (WEAVING) WEIGHT TZ 1.49

6.5 Rolling pin and door-hinge

Finally, special mention should be made of a few items related to house-building: a basalt door-hinge stone of the pivot type (Fig. 6.4) and a small basalt rolling pin which apparently was used to finish plastered walls from TZ 2.54 (Fig 5.5:14), diam. 50 or 49 mm, width 81 mm.[17] Unfortunately, the door-hinge was not found in situ.[18] It was probably a lower door-hinge. The socket in which the door pivoted was not very deep. The groove at the side of the door socket could be a sign of wear or, perhaps, it was deliberately made to secure the door when closed.

---

[9] The closest parallel which I found was in Yahalom-Mack, 2007, 640-641; Photo 11.2, Fig. 11.1:11.

[10] See Ibrahim, 1976, Pl. XXXIII 227 (Area B).

[11] One of unknown provenance is shown on a photo with the door-hinge stone (Fig. 6:4); perhaps it was a piece of undressed natural stone or a fossil with an original perforation.

[12] Yaholam-Mack, 2007, Reg. 189061 who thinks of MB mace heads.

[13] This whorl seems unfinished. It is uncompletely perforated, see also Yahalom-Mack, 2007, 661, Nos 1 and 3.

[14] Of these spindle whorls, only those from TZ 1.54 and 2.51 were made of limestone.

[15] Rowe, 1940, Pl. XXVII, 8–9; James and McGovern, 1993; 194–195, Fig. 127:12–13; Yadin, 1956 (Hazor II), Pl. 127:2–21; Harrison, 2004 (Megiddo 3), 376, Fig. 11.8 3–5; Chambon, 1984, Pl. 76:9–11; Dever, 1986 (Gezer IV), Pl. 49:1; Yahalom-Mack, 2007, 651-652.

[16] Mortin, 1999, 182, No. 129.

[17] Different from the common heavy rolling-pins that were used for large horizontal surfaces such as the roof and floor. King and Stager, 2001, 24, 29.

[18] As BAI Wuppertal did in the southern Early Iron House in Area 1, Vieweger and Häser, 2007b, 155; Rowe, 1940, Pl. XXVII, 11.

FIG 6.4 DOOR-HINGE AND WEAVING WEIGHT (?)

Findno. and stratum	Description of find spot	Description of object and context	Figures
1 B	Surface find	No further information	
2.6 / I.3	Yellow earth E. of W6, cf. 1.7	Millstone	
2.9 / I.2	Wall W1	Upper millstone black basalt	
2.10 / I.3	Wall W6	Reused lower basalt millstone	
1.26 / II.1	Wall W7	Ceramic spindlewhorl	Fig 5.5:9
2.29 / II.1	Lower stones of Wall W7	Fragment of large lower millstone with ribbed surface	Fig 6:1
2.30 / II.1	Red-brown earth under Wall W7 west of Wall W 12	Millstone	
1.29 / III.1	Red-brown earth under millstone in Wall W7	Broken millstone, related to Floor Fl.E?	
2.15 / III.1	Red earth east of Wall W1	Millstone	
2.26 / III.3	Red-brown earth with grits and gravel, below TZ 2.23, deposit on ash layer (cf. TZ 1.35; 2.35)	Millstone	
1.46 / IV.5	Fill of Pit P2a: ash, rubble, mud bricks	Millstone	
1.46 / IV.5	Fill of Pit P2a: ash, rubble, mud bricks	Limestone weaving weight or rolling-pin diam. 55 mm, width 65 mm; partly broken	Fig 5.5:12
1.48 / IV.5	Fill of Pit 2b: yellowish soil washed down, Wall W18 in SW. quarter	Three millstones	
1.49 / IV 5	Fill of Pit P2a: with broken bricks and ash	Basalt weaving weight	Fig 5.5:18; 6.3
1.49 / IV 5	Fill of Pit P2a: with broken bricks and ash	Ceramic spindlewhorl	Fig 5.5:10
1.54 / IV.5	Firepit in fill of Pit P2b	Limestone spindlewhorl	Fig 5.5:8
1.59 / IV 5	Fill of Pit P2b	Bowllike mortar of grey vesicular basalt 270 mm x 231 mm x 170 mm	Fig 6.2
1.59 / IV 5	Fill of Pit P2b	Small trapozoid pestle	Fig 5.5:13; Fig 6.2
1.59 / IV 5	Fill of Pit P2b	Rim of black basalt bowl diam. 22	Fig 5.5:16
1.61 / IV 5	Fill of Pit P2b	Ceramic spindlewhorl	Fig 5.5:11
2.45 / IV.3	Stones western continuation of Wall W16?	Part of black basalt mortar, polished inside (+) 2.49? diam. 32 rim diam. 22 base	Fig 5.5:17
2.49 / 0.0-IV.3	Under TZ 2.47 on accumulation of stone mixed with surface finds	Part of black basalt mortar, polished inside (+) 2.45?; pestle and a millstone	Fig 5.5:17
2.51 / IV.5	Pit P3, locus of Iron Age[?] pithos in fill under TZ 2.50	Limestone spindle whorl	
2.52 / IV.3	Floor Fl.J	Weavingweight	Fig 5.5:15
2.54 / IV.3	Wall W13	Basalt roller diam 50/49 mm width 81 mm; its has on either side an undeep hollow.	Fig 5.5:14
2.56 / IV.4	Floor Fl.K and down to stone deposit below (S. half)	Large lower millstone of black basalt *in situ* in Floor Fl.K	
2.58 / IV.5	Pit P3, fill below TZ 2.50–51	Millstone	
1.51 / V.2	Yellowish soil under TZ 1.48	Ceramic spindlewhorl	Fig 5.5:7
1.60 / V.2	Wall W19, core and W. of it yellowish loamy soil, bricks	Millstone	
1.62 / V.2	Solid yellowish loamy soil	Millstone	

Table 6.2 Stone implements.

During the campaigns at Tall Zar^{c}a (TZ) in the autumn of 2001 and of 2002, rich finds of hearths and cooking facilities were discovered in the rather small area of the sondage (6 m × 6 m) on the west side of the plateau of the tell. The sondage revealed parts of houses from different Iron Age periods (1A, IA/B-IIA and IIB). This area appeared to have been inhabited and used for preparation of daily food in Iron Age I–IIB and in Roman–Byzantine times. An assortment of kitchen utensils like millstones, pestles and mortars, tanānīr and hearths were recovered. Even an imploded but nearly complete Iron Age cooking pot was found in situ, on a shallow pit with ash. Cooking pot sherds were found in substantial numbers all over the Iron Age strata.[1]

7.1 Introduction.

In a preliminary study,[2] the first counts of these sherds were used to look for statistical correlations between standard parameters of cooking pots. One remarkable result was the relationship between cumulative rim length in centimetres per TZ Findno. and recovered cooking pot surface area in square centimetres per Findno. for small samples. This correlation, then, could be described by an exponential curve[3] and compiled to a simulation matrix of curves only by changing rim circumference and corresponding mean cooking pot surface area. This mathematical model was chosen in the first place in order to compare dated cooking pot repertoires of other archaeological sites (e.g. Tall Dayr ^{c}Allā[4]) with our own repertoire from Tall Zar^{c}a as a try-out of dating the stratigraphy of the sondage early in our studies. In the second place, it was to assess the variance of size or, in other words, to resolve whether we were dealing with a pluriform or a uniform repertoire. Graph 7.2 shows it to be uniform.

Eventually, a statistical 'fingerprint' of the repertoire could be traced out from the number of recovered cooking pot sherds and the uniformity of their original size. Later, after the stratigraphy of the sondage was firmly established from the strata, new counts were made to check the earlier data which had been based on the preliminary stratigraphy (Table 7.1, right column). Cumulating the counts the data for rim length and

recovered surface areas of cooking pots shifted from the first exponential curve[5] into a more linear correlation (see Graph 7.1). However, surprisingly, the proportional relation between original surface area and circumference of pots did not completely disappear. This result is quite remarkable but probably inherent to the large numbers of collected sherds and to the uniform composition of the TZ repertoire (little variance in diameter). After so many centuries, only a 5% of the original cooking pots in this test trench were recovered, but in spite of such a degree of degradation, what was recovered contained still a quantitative indication of the original mean ratio of surface area to 1 m rim length of the pots 0,16 m^2 ± 0,04 m^2.

Mean values	Population $N=$ 201 2002	Population $N=$ 242 2008
Length of rim	5,7 cm	6,0 cm
Circumference of rim, 2p	34,2 cm ± 8 cm	36,0 cm ± 8 cm
Height of ornamental rim, h_r	2,2 cm	2,1 cm
Height of carination on rim, h_c	?	5,1 cm
Height of vertical break in rim	?	4,0 cm
Surface area of rim, $(h_r \times 2\pi\rho)/4 = kl$	57,0 cm^2	56,5 cm^2
Height of cooking pot, h	20,5 cm ± 2 cm	19 cm ± 2 cm
Surface area of cooking pot, $\pi(h^2 + \rho^2)$	0,22 m^2	0,22 m^2
c is constante. c × mean area ckp	(1,0 ± 0,3)/ m^2 0,16 m^2 – 0,28 m^2 (the range in size of ckp)	(1,0 ± 0,3)/ m^2
Circumference of rim, $2\pi\rho$	107,3 cm	112,0 cm
Ratio of Rim circumference to mean rim length	19	19

Table 7.1. Means of various measurements of the rim of cooking pot sherds.[6]

---

[1] Table 7.6 Cooking pot data according to strata (substrata) January 2009.
[2] Dijkstra, Dijkstra, Vriezen, 2005, 180-182.
[3] $a - x = k_1 \times e^{c \times 0.22 \times N}$ where (a – x) is the recovered surface area of sherds in cm^2; $k_1 = (h_1 \times 2\pi \times \rho)/4$ where h_1 is the height of the rim in cm and 2ρ the diameter of the ckp in cm ; N is the number of rim sherds for each locus and 0.22 the mean surface area in m^2. c = 1.0 ± 0.3/m^2 and describes the variance of surface area. In this study c = 1.0/m^2.
[4] Franken and Kalsbeek, 1969.

---

[5] Footnote 2.
[6] Dijkstra, Dijkstra, Vriezen, 2005, 180-182.

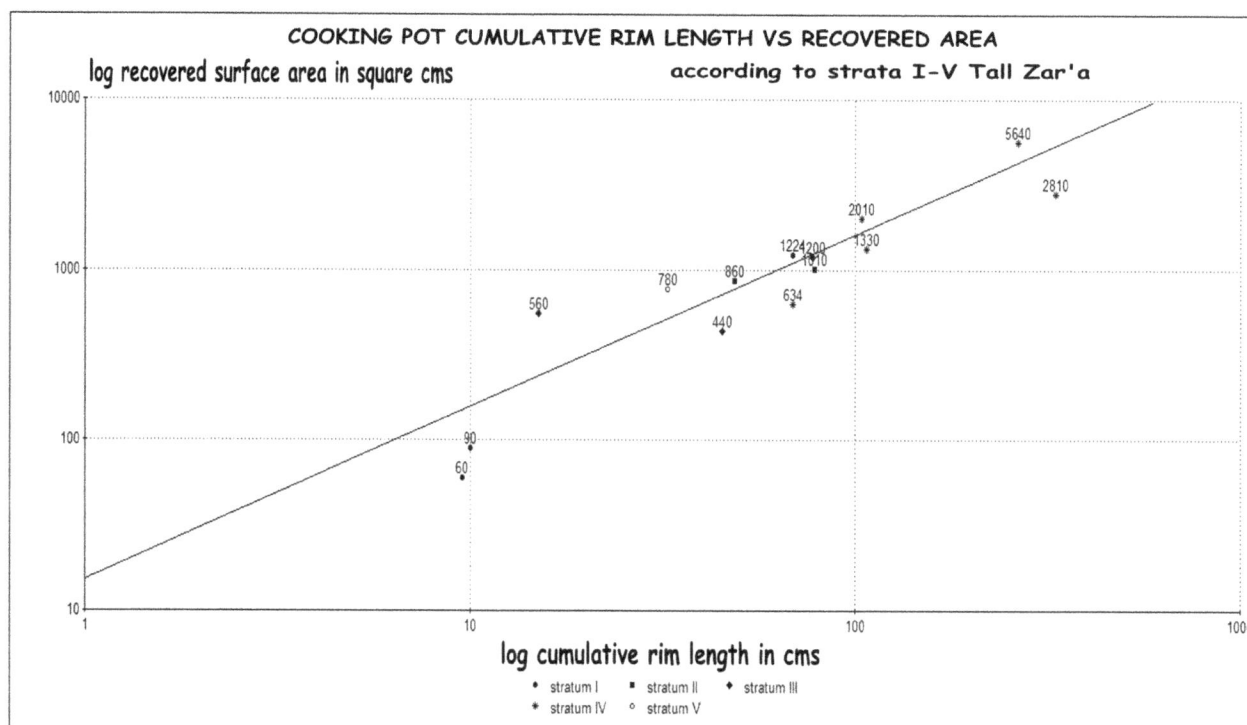

Graph 7.1 Cumulative data on cooking pots from Field 1 and 2 of Tall Zar^{c}a for each stratum/substratum (I-V), $N = 14$. The linear slope (coefficient) of area to length of rim fragments is 0,16 m^2 ± 0,04 m^2 (Table 7.6).

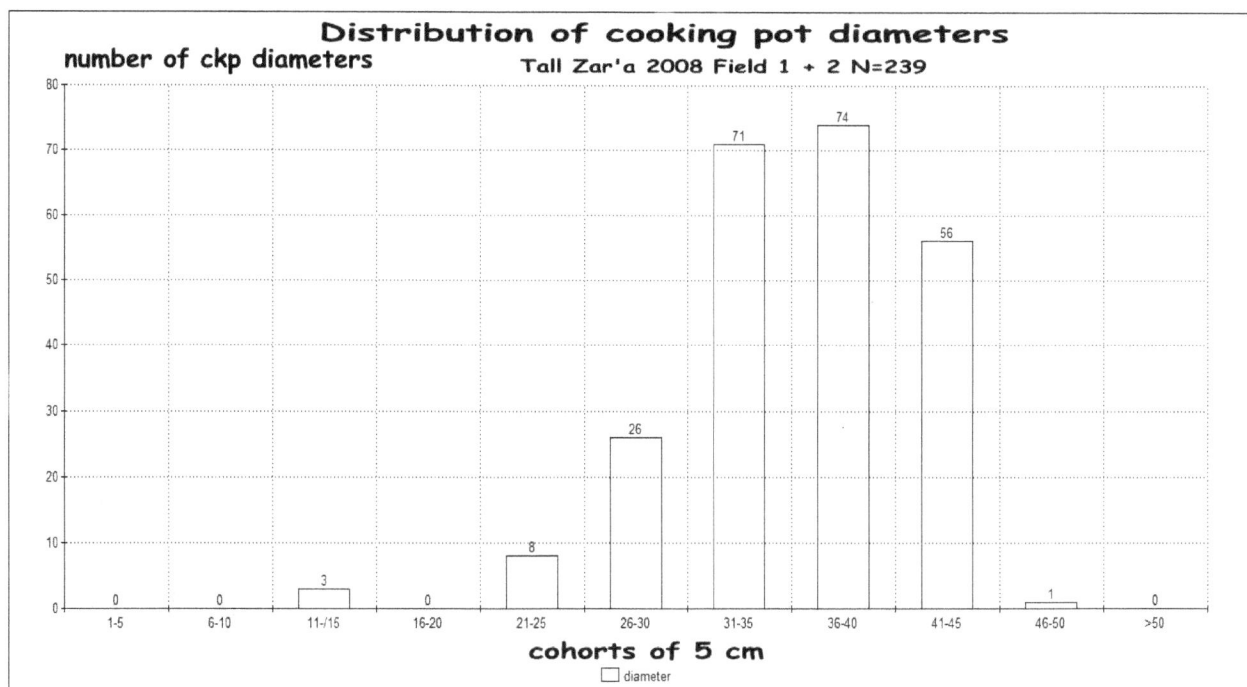

Graph 7.2 Frequency diagram of diameter of cooking pots. The mean diameter is 36 cm. The modus 38 cm. The distribution is unimodal with slight skewness to the left. Appearance of cooking jugs and smaller shapes during Iron Age II.

7.2 Results.

In a further archaeometric analysis, the cooking pots found in the sondage, were compared with other ceramic types (jars, bowls, chalices, cups etc.) of the Iron Age. Tables 7.2–4 survey the proportion of diagnostic sherds to other types of ceramic. It is quite surprising to see the overwhelming presence of cooking pot fragments. Table 7.6 presents an example of the data used for Tables 7.2–4 and Graph 7.1. Most of the derived types and sizes of the cooking pots are based on reconstruction, measurements of the curvature, decoration style, rim section, carination and thickness of rim fragments. Based on the section of the rim, a classification of three types was made and the classes subdivided into twelve evolutionary classes (Graph 7.3 and Graph 7.4). About 40% of the cooking pots were types of the Late Bronze IIB / Iron Age IA period and 55% were of Iron Age IA–B. The remaining 5% were IA IIA and 1% Late Bronze II. See for the different types also Fig. 4.7 and 4.8:20-22, 27,28.

The usual cooking pot had a convex bowl shaped curvature with strong angular carination and an as a 'fir-tree' folded rim (Fig. 4.7:9; 4.16; 7.1). The average rim diameter was 36 cm ± 8 cm, the height 19 cm ± 2 cm and surface area 0,22 m^2 ± 0,06 m^2. No cooking pots with handles were found. Nevertheless a few cooking jugs were excavated and reconstructed (Fig. 4.5:15; 7.2). The production of cooking pots must have been high-rated to compensate for the losses caused by repeated heating of the vulnerable bases of cooking pots. Most of the cooking pots were probably made in local potteries but the clay types used could not be analysed for lack of characteristic mineralogical information of the Gadara region.[7] The traditional wide-mouthed cooking pot of Late Bronze IIB / Iron Age IA occurring frequently among the TZ

ceramics, was made in two stages: the lower part (base / body) in a mould, and the upper part (body/shoulder /neck) by adding clay coils by hand and finishing with slow turning tables (tournettes). Between the lower and the upper part, there may be an angular carination.

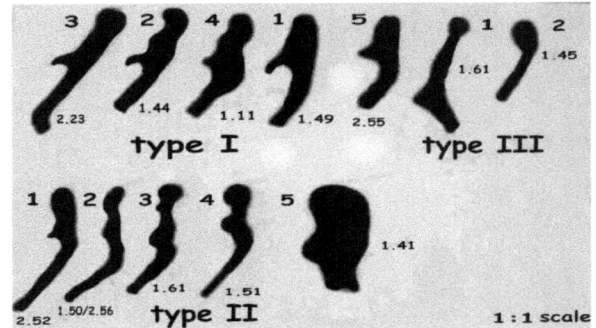

Graph 7.4 Types of rim sherds of cooking pots by section profile arranged by Findnos. Three types and twelve subtypes could be discerned and compared with the classifications of Franken and Dornemann.[8]

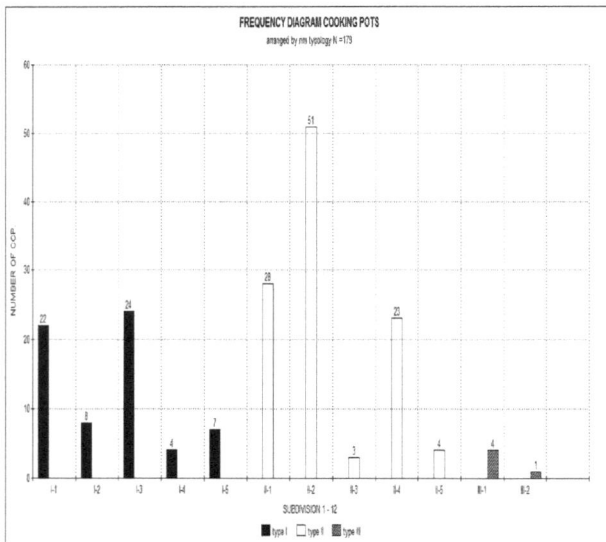

FIG. 7.1 – IRON AGE I COOKINGPOT (TZ 2.33) STRATUM IV = TYPE I

FIG. 7.2: AN IRON AGE I COOKING JUG (AMPHORA) TZ 2.54

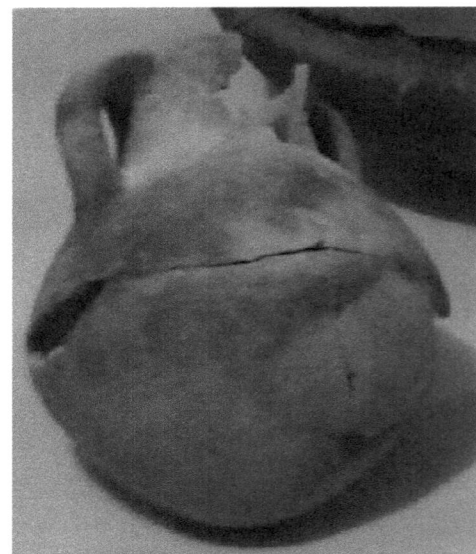

Graph 7.3 Distribution of cooking pots from Tall Zarᶜa by rim typology. Type I is Late Bronze / Iron Age IA; Type II is Iron Age IA–B; Type III is Iron Age I-IIA (see Graph 7.4).

---

[7] Vieweger and Häser, 2005, 15-16.

[8] Franken and Kalsbeek, 1969, 119–126. Dornemann, 1983, 217-218,Figs 24-25 with Sequence I.

7.3 Comparing Iron Age cooking pot finds.

A survey of the development of the cooking pot in Iron Age Cis-Jordan and Transjordan is summarized and compared with the Tall Zarᶜa findings in Table 7.5. From the Late Bronze to the successive Iron Age periods the changes in design are at first conservative. That is also true for Tall Zarᶜa. It is difficult to make a distinction between Late Bronze IIB and Iron Age IA. There is much tradition in pottery making and a conservative approach in using different sizes of one and the same type cooking pot for different kinds of food preparation. With new imports and changing needs for food preparation from Iron Age II onwards, the overall shape and size became more differentiated. From improvements in pot-making skills and better production methods, new traditions and forms may have originated. The following trends (classified 1 to 5) express a sort of an evolutionary track during the Iron Age:

1. Decreasing diameter cooking pot from 34 cm (Fig. 7.1, type I) to 28 cm (Type II) to 16-19 cm (Type III) to 8–12 cm (for a cooking jug).
2. Enlargment of the shoulder and decrease of carination. Appearence of handles at rim and shoulder.
3. Decrease in size and height of the rim. Angular triangle rim and the convex neck become less frequent and profiled. The bowl-shaped body changes to a spherical shape (the ratio diameter / height of 1,5 becomes equal and finally 0,4 in cooking jugs).
4. Cooking pot-making with a mould and a tournette is superseded by throwing on the fast-turning potter's wheel. This evolution is reflected in changes in breakage pattern from vertical breaks at the rim to oblique breaks.
5. Less finger imprints, more traces of turning. Thickness of the wall tends to become more equal all over the body. The body tends to become harder and to produce a more metallic sound when knocked. Non-plastic inclusions become smaller.

In the repertoire of the Tall Zarᶜa sondage only trends 1.-3. are commonly present.

7.4 Summarizing Iron Age cooking pots from the sondage.

The cooking pots from the sondage are quite impressive in number but less so in the general development of cooking pot types during the Iron Age. The size of the cooking pots remained moderate and over time they varied little in design. The collection, though uniform, is useful in its remarkable number of sherds from a restricted area, so that another archaeometric approach was also interesting, namely an approach to prediction of ceramic loss in the course of time. The mathematical compartment model, which describes the rate of disappearance of ceramic artefacts in the course of time,

was worked out in the first report of cooking pot finds.[9] It aim was to understand what happens after the pot breaks, or is worn out and discarded. The process of loss in the course of time has always been considered as being one of both *continuity* (by natural weathering processes) and *discontinuity* (by sudden events like earthquakes and heavy rainfall), but sherds seem to behave like molecules disappearing at a geometric rate (the same fraction disappearing in a given time) from one compartment to another.

Two important outcomes of this model for archaeometric research are the following: a predictable recovery index of any ceramic artefacts in the course of time and an amazing statistical preservation of original proportions of any ceramic type, provided the sherd samples are large enough and the population of the investigated types are reasonably uniform. In the sondage's repertoire, the recovery index was found to be about 5%, with a mean circumference of 112,0 cm and a mean diameter of 36,0 cm. The calculated surface area based on these parameters, was 0,22 m^2 and the statistically deduced value 0.16 m^2 ± 0,04 m^2 (Graph 7.1). The cooking pot repertoire of Tall Zarᶜa does not differ much from repertoires such as that of Tall Dayr ᶜAllā. Both have a specific Transjordanian touch. The share of the cooking pots in the total Iron Age ceramic repertoire was ca 20% (Table 7.2), but almost 40% on the basis of diagnostic sherds (Table 7.3).

---

[9] Dijkstra, Dijkstra, Vriezen, 2005, 180-182.

Table 7.2 Number and proportion of different types of Iron Age sherds, Tall Zar°a 2008.

Type/ Sherd	Cooking pots	Large bowl / Crater	Small bowl	Cup / Chalice	Jug / Juglet	Storage Jar /Collared-rim Jar	Indefinite	Total
Rim	220 21 %	86 8,2 %	64 6,1 %	56 5,3 %	62 5,9 %	53 6,1 %	3 0,3 %	544
Profile	33 3,2 %	5 0,5 %	5 0,5 %	2 0,2 %	21 2,0 %	41 3,9 %	33 3,2 %	140
Bottom	2 0,2 %	31 3,0 %	4 0,4 %	3 0,3 %	17 1,6 %	68 6,5 %	0	125
Handle	0	1 0,1 %	0	0 0 %	21 2,0 %	216 20,6 %	0	238
Total	255 24,4 %	123 11,7 %	73 6,9 %	61 5,0 %	121 11,6 %	378 36,1 %	36 3,4 %	1047 100 %

Table 7.3 Number and proportion of rims from different types of Iron Age pottery.

Cooking pot	Large bowl / Crater	Small bowl	Cup / Chalice	Jug / Juglet	Storage Jar / Collared-Rim Jar	Indefinite	Total
220	86	64	56	62	53	3	544
40,4 %	15,8 %	11,8 %	10,3 %	11,2 %	9,7 %	0,6 %	100 %

Table 7.4 Number and proportion of Iron Age sherds from cooking pots and other pottery types.

Stratigraphic elements	Number of body sherds from cooking pots	Number of body sherds from other pottery types	Total number of sherds	Proportion of sherds from cooking pots
Counts of stratigraphic elements from Strata 1B / 2B to 1,25/2,15 (not counted in 2002)	147	784	931 (Nov. 2005)	15,8 %
Stratigraphic elements 1,26 to 1,62 and 2,16 to 2,56	1223	4739	5962 (October 2002)	20,5 %

Table 7.5 Chronological classification[10] of cooking pots: comparing different cooking pot typologies from Cisjordan and Transjordan with the Tall Zarʻa finds.

Chronology	13–12th C.	12–11th C.	11–10th C.	10–8th C.	End 8th/start of 6th C.	Excavation area
Trend in Typology	Standard/ Baseline	1	2	3	4	
Franken and Kalsbeek, 1969, 118-132	Late Bronze II	Type I A–D Type II E–H[11]	Type II. J–M Type III[12] G-L	Cooking jug?		Transjordan: Dayr ʻAllā
Amiran 1970 227–232, Pls. 75–76	Canaanite proto-type	Iron Age I	Iron Age I / II A–B	Iron Age II A–B / C		North: Megiddo Hazor Samaria
idem				Iron Age II A–B	Iron Age IIC / Cooking jug	South: Beth Shemesh / Lachish, Ein Gedi, Arad
Dornemann 1983, 218, 234	LB II <	Sequence I Type I and II	>> Type III	> <	Sequence II	Transjordan
Vilders 1992, 162; idem, 1993, 149–156		A1	A2	B / Cook- ing jug	>	Transjordan: Tell es- Saʻidayeh
Dijkstra et al. 2001 / 2002	LB II? > Tall Zarʻa Type I	Tall Zarʻa Type I / II h = 4,0 cm –3,3 cm? <IA II h = 2,4 cm –2,0 cm	< Tall Zarʻa Type II h =1,8 cm ? >> Type III cooking jug >			Transjordan Tall Zarʻa
Period	Late Bronze IIB	Iron Age IA	Iron Age IB	Iron Age IIA,B	Iron Age IIC	

---

[10] For practical reasons, the chronology of the Iron Age is based on centuries. The symbol h is the height of the rim. The symbols < and > stand for fluent transition periods.

[11] The variant DA type IIg is closely related to Late Bronze type II (Franken).

[12] DA- type III is probably a smaller variant DA- type II and not yet developed to a cooking jug.

Table 7.6 Cooking pot data according to strata (substrata): Tall Zar^{c}a.

Findnr Field 1	Findnr Field 2	Stratum/ substratum	number rimfragm Field 1	Number rimfrag Field 2	Cum. Length Rimfrag Field cm	Cum. Length rimfrag Field 2 cm	Recovered area ccp Field 1 cm2	Recovered Area ccp Field 2 cm2
		I I.1						
IB	2B	-						
	2.18							
Tot. B								
I.1			2		9.5		60	
Tot. I.1			2		9.5		60	
		I I.2						
1.2	2.2			2		3		60
1.3	2.3		1		4		0	
1.4	2.5							
1.5	2.9							
1.6	2.16	?						
1.17			1		3		30	
Tot. I.2			2	2	7	3	30	60
Fld 1 and 2				4		10		90
		I I.3						
1.7	2.4		4		26.5		490	
1.8	2.6			2				
1.9	2.7		1		1.5		180	
1.10	2.8			1		4.5	20	30
1.11	2.10		4	3	25.5	3	330	60
1.12			1				0	
1.15	2.13		1		5		80	30
	2.20			1		3		4
Tot. I.3			11	7	58.5	10.5	1100	124
Fld 1 and 2				18		69		1224
		II II.1						
1.13	2.17						100	
1.18	2.19							90
1.19							90	
1.20	2.24		1	1	1.5	6	120	30
1.22	2.27							
1.23	2.29		1		9		70	

Findnr Field 1	Findnr Field 2	Stratum/ substratum	number rimfragm Field 1	Number rimfrag Field 2	Cum. Length Rimfrag Field 1	Cum. Length rimfrag Field 2	Recovered area ccp Field 1 cm2	Recovered Area ccp Field 2 cm2
	2.30			3		17.5		240
1.26			2		6.5		60	
1.41			2		8		60	
Tot. II.1			6	4	25	23.5	500	360
Fld 1 and 2				10		48.5		860
		II II.2						
	2.21			1		3		80
1.24	2.25		9		6.5		300	
1.25	2.28		8	8	37.5	26.5	370	260
	2.35			1		5		
Tot. II.2			17	10	44	34.5	670	340
Fld 1 and 2				27		78.5		1010
		III III.1						
1.14	2.11			3		3		60
1.16	2.12		2	1	13.5	3.5	190	70
1.21	2.14		2	1	8	4	160	120
1.27	2.15		3	2	17	4	90	80
1.28	2.22		1	2	3	16.5	170	130
1.29								
1.30			1		5		130	
1.31								
Tot. III III.1			9	9	46.5	31	740	460
Fld 1 And 2				18		77.5		1200
		III III.2						
	2.23			3		13.5		150
1.32	2.36		1	5	5	26.5	30	260
Tot. III.2			1	8	5	40	30	410
Fld 1 and 2				9		45		440
		III III.3						
1.35	2.26		1	1	3	7	320	240
	2.35		1			5		
Tot. III.3			2	1	3	12	320	240
Fld 1 and 2				3		15		560

Findnr Field 1	Findnr Field 2	Stratum/ substratum	number rimfragm Field 1	Number rimfrag Field 2	Cum. Length Rimfrag Field 1	Cum. Length rimfrag Field 2	Recovered area ccp Field 1 cm2	Recovered Area ccp Field 2 cm2
		IV IV.1						
1.40								
Tot IV.1			0	0	0	0	0	0
		IV IV.2						
1.37	2.31		2	9	12	39	90	320
1.38	2.32		1		3.5		4	
1.39	2.33			1		5		90
1.34								
	2.44			2		9.5		130
	2.46							
Tot. IV.2			3	12	15.5	53..5	94	540
Fld 1 and 2				15		69		634
		IV IV.3						
1.42	2.37		9	5	44.5	22.5	480	160
	2.38			4		45		320
	2.39			8		48.5		290
1.45	2.40		3		13		80	10
	2.41							
	2.42							
	2.43							
	2.45							
	2.47			2		6		10
	2.49			4		22		290
	2.52			5		26.5		390
	2.53			1		10		110
	2.54			5		60		390
	2.55			4		22.5		140
	2.34			3		10.5		140
Tot. IV.3			12	41	57.5	273.5	560	2250
Fld.1 and 2				53		331		2810
		IV IV.4						
	2.56			15		91		1910
	2.57			2		13		100
Tot. IV.4				17		104		2010
		IV IV.5a						

Findnr Field 1	Findnr Field 2	Stratum/ substratum	number rimfragm Field 1	Number rimfrag Field 2	Cum. Length Rimfrag Field 1	Cum. Length rimfrag Field 2	Recovered area ccp Field 1 cm2	Recovered Area ccp Field 2 cm2
1.43			6		25		150	
1.44			1		4		40	
1.46			5		21.5		180	
1.47								
1.48			2		10		20	
1.49			20		113.5		4310	
1.50			14		91		940	
Tot. IV.5a			48		265		5640	
		IV IV.5b						
1.52	2.50			1		4.5	20	80
1.53	2.51							
1.54	2.58							
1.59			6		29		430	
1.61			10		73.5		800	
Tot. IV.5 b			16	1	102.5	4.5	1250	80
Fld1 and 2				17		107		1330
		V V.1						
		V V.2						
1.51	2.48		3		14.5		570	
1.55	2.59		1	2	5	13	50	100
1.56								
1.57								
1.58								
1.60								
1.62							60	
Tot. V.2			4	2	19.5	13	680	100
Fld 1 and 2				6		32.5		780

CHAPTER 8

TALL ZARᶜA = GADARA IN THE LATER BRONZE AND EARLY IRON AGE

8.1 Canaan as an Egyptian province during the New Kingdom

A survey of the site of Tall Zarᶜa and its surroundings in Wādī al-ᶜArab produced clear evidence of occupation in the Late Bronze and Early Iron Ages. The survey included pilot surveys in 2001–2002 and campaigns of excavation by the Biblisch Archäologisches Institut (BAI) Wuppertal (2003–2008) at the tell itself. In particular, BAI found casemate walls and other fortifications of the Late Bronze Age at the NW edge of the tell.[1] It was a significant fortified town from the second half of the 2ⁿᵈ Millennium BCE, along a route from the Jordan Valley through the Wādī al-ᶜArab to the Transjordan Plateau and one would expect it to be mentioned in written sources from the period. The road through Wādī al-ᶜArab provided an easy approach to southern Syria, passing the fords in the Yarmūk Estuary at Tall al-Shihāb or Darᶜā.[2]

During most of the Late Bronze Period, the southern areas of the Levant – usually known as Canaan but in Egyptian sources also named Djahi, Lower Rethenu or Khuru – were a sort of colony, if not a province, of the New Kingdom. Biblical tradition preserves a memory of this in grouping Canaan together with Misraim (Egypt), Cush (Nubia) and Put (Gen.10:6). In a series of campaigns which took them repeatedly to Qadesh at the Orontes and further at the banks of the Euphrates, the 18ᵗʰ Dynasty pharaohs Tuthmosis I, Thutmosis III and Amenophis II secured the area south of the line Byblos (Nahr el-Kalb), Kamid el-Loz (Kumidi) and Damascus in the inland province of Upe and, with varying fortunes, this situation of Egyptian occupation and administration was maintained until the reign of Ramesses III of the 20ᵗʰ Dynasty and perhaps even after him.

The extensive topographical lists of Tuthmosis III and presumably also those of Amenophis II represent slightly different versions of a system of itineraries and military bases concentrated in the coastal area of northern Palestine, around the Lake Kinneret, Jordan and South Syria between the Yarmūk Estuary and Damascus in the province of Upe. Though not every detail of their arrangement is transparent, it was especially intended to control the approaches to the regions and borders of northern Canaan and southern Syria. There we find the majority of bases securing Egyptian rule in this area of the Levant.

Despite the propaganda of their war inscriptions, it is far from certain whether Tuthmosis III or one of his successors ever fully controlled their 'Northern Province', Upper Rethenu, though some of them adorned their inscriptions with extensive topographical lists featuring subdued countries and conquered cities in this region. Egypt certainly showed her presence there at irregular intervals and even collected tribute from the princes of Amurru, Ugarit, Qatna and other Syrian kingdoms. These cities may have been in her sphere of political influence and some cities such as Byblos, Sumur, Qatna and Qadesh / Kinza nursed strong ties with Egypt. Though many historiographical essays on Syria included the entire country of Amurru and its surroundings in the 'northern province' of the Egyptian Empire, firm evidence for Egyptian territorial claims in the area come only from a few sites such as Sumur, Tunip and Qadesh / Kinza.[3] Perhaps with the exception of Sumur,[4] the Pharaonic claims do not indicate that they set up a permanent administration supported by military garrisons and fortresses as they did in the provinces Lower Rethenu / Canaan (including Sinai) and Upe. Horemheb did not reclaim the lost strongholds in Syria either, though his campaigns took 'Egypt' once again from Byblos to Karkemish in order to quell the political upheavals in the Levant in the aftermath of the Amarna Period.[5]

8.2 Gadara during the 19ᵗʰ Dynasty

Seti I – as co-regent of his ageing father Ramesses I, the actual successor to Horemheb – continued these political and military ambitions in his first regnal year as sole ruler.[6] A splendid summary of this campaign we find depicted on the eastern side of the North Wall of the

---

[1] See in addition to the preliminary reports in Dijkstra *et al.*, 2005, Vieweger and Häser, 2007a, 1–27; Vieweger and Häser, 2007b, 151–165.

[2] Not only the stela of Seti I from Tell al-Shihāb found long ago (1901), but also the recently discovered fragment of a stela of Ramesses II, found reused in a wall of the mosque in al-Turrah a few miles south of Tell al-Shihāb, seems to mark one of the main roads taken by commerce and armies from the Jordan Valley into Southern Syria and beyond. By courtesy of Dr Wajeeh Karasneh, director on the Department of Antiquities in Irbid, I was shown photographs of the al-Turrah inscription in November 2006. It is the lower left corner of a basalt stele with the remains of cartouches of Ramesses II as also found in the stele from Tyre of the 4ᵗʰ Year. The inscription will be published bij Stefan Wimmer, who kindly provided me with a copy of his forthcoming article. About the stele of Ramesses II from Sheikh Saᶜad (the Stone of Job), see below.

[3] Murnane, 1990, 4–21;139–144.

[4] Murnane, 1990, 4.

[5] His campaign was probably related to the revolts in that area against the Hittite rule *ca* 1315 BCE. See the bowl of Sen-Nefer in *TUAT 1/6*, 540–1; Redford, 1992, 177.

[6] About the problems of dating Seti I's campaigns, see Murnane, 1990, 74–94; Hasel, 1998, 119-124.

Great Hall or Hypostyle in the Temple of Amun at Karnak. The attack and conquest of the city of Yanu^cam there illustrated corresponds with the campaign as described and commemorated on the larger stele of Year 1 discovered at the site of ancient Beth Shean (Tell el-Husn, Tel Bet She'an):

> On this day, someone came to speak to His Majesty: "The wretched foe who is in the town of Hammat has gathered many people around him in order to seize the town of Beth Shean. He has made a pact with the people of Pahil (Pella) and will not allow the prince of Rehob to go outside." Thereupon His Majesty sent from his first army the division of 'Amun, the Mighty Archer' to the town of Hammat, from his first army the division of 'Re, Plentiful of Courage' to the town of Beth-Shean and from his first army the division of 'Seth, the Strong Archer' to the town of Yanu'am. Not a day had passed before they were defeated by the glory of His Majesty ... [7]

Seti I seems to have used this 'normal' local contest between vassals, which the Egyptian suzerains had previously usually ignored,[8] as a pretext to reinstate the military base of Beth Shean for his own future plans to restore Egyptian order in surrounding areas and to revive old territorial claims. He apparently interfered in this local war between the rulers of Hammat and Pahil (Pella) on the one hand and those of Beth Shean and Rehob (Tell el-Sarem = Tel Rehov)[9] on the other, because it was a contest about the control of the fords in the Jordan River, in particular the road running through the Valley of Beth Shean and after crossing the Jordan River and leading to the plateau of Transjordan and southern Syria.

Seti I did not take half measures. Though the inscriptions are rhetorical and ostentatious, it may be assumed that they also offer some insights into sound military strategy. After securing the coastal approach in southern Palestine against the Shosu, the first army, apparently composed of three divisions, was divided into three task forces, one of which was left as a garrison at Beth Shean,[10] while the other two secured the roads and borders to the north on both sides of Lake Kinneret and the River Jordan (Fig. 8.2). The mentioning of Yanu^cam as a target in this context is of interest because it does not seem to be a party to this local conflict. Renewed conquest would be in Seti's own interest. Na^caman rightly stressed the status of Yanu^cam as an Egyptian garrison like Beth Shean and Kumudi (Tell Kamid el-Loz, Rift Valley in southernmost

Lebanon).[11] It explains also the prominent place of Yanu^cam in the battle reliefs in Karnak. Though Yanu^cam is quite often mentioned in Egyptian texts, especially in topographical lists of the New Kingdom and once in an Amarna letter (EA 197) sent by Biryawaza, ruler of Damascus, the site of Yanu^cam has not been identified conclusively. Clauß suggested Tell an-Na^cameh in the Huleh Valley some 10 km south-west of Tell el-Qadi (Tel Dan), but others have proposed sites in the Jordan Valley south of Lake Kinneret. However, a site near Beth Shean, west of the Jordan, is not compatible with the evidence. Looking for a site in Transjordan on the periphery of the Bashan Region, Na^caman suggested Tell al-Shihab. Though I agree with his line of argument, I think a position in the Yarmūk Valley at the site of Tell al-Shihāb is still too far south-east into the Bashan Region. Because of topographical associations with known cities and regions such as Tahsi in Syria and Lebanon and the 'context' of the Palestinian battle reliefs from Seti I and Merenptah,[12] a situation in the Upper Jordan Valley or in the area between southern Lebanon and Syria is provisionally a better option, that is: the Clauß–Albright identification.[13] A toponym Yanu^cam is not attested in the Old Testament, but one may surmise that Yanoah in 2 Kings 15:29 is a corruption or variant of this toponym, perhaps accidently harmonized with the town of Yanoah* (locative < Yanoha) in the description of the Ephraim–Manasse border (Josh. 16:6-7; Onom. 108, 20-21).[14]

Tuthmosis III took the same road on his way to the north setting up a stele, of which a fragment was discovered at Khirbet el-^cOremeh (Kinneret?).[15] Because the immediate threat came from the other side of the Jordan, according to the larger Beth Shean stele of Seti I, an obvious choice would be to send one of the divisions – actually the Amun division – against Hammat and Pahil (Pella). A direct though silent witness that Seti I pacified cities in the Yarmūk Estuary, is the stele found at Tell al-Shihāb.[16] Unfortunately only the upper part has survived in which Seti I is depicted in front of Amun-Re, Lord of Heaven, Lord of the Two Lands and the goddess Mut. The scene

---

[7] The stele was often partly translated, ANET[3], 253-254; Murnane, 1990, 42-43; for recent treatment and discussion, see Kitchen, 2000, 25-26 and Werning, 2005.

[8] Murnane, 1990, 13.

[9] This identification is now taken for granted. However, Schumacher 1885/1890, Steuernagel 1925 found evidence for an ancient road passing through the Wādī al-^cArab along Bayt Rās/Capitolias to al-Turrah (and another branch to Dar'ā) passing through Kh. Rahūb (Cv Roob). *JADIS* 1994 and Mittmann 1970 noted only Early Bronze sherds lying next to a large enclosure (148x80x5), which seemingly has not been investigated yet.

[10] The renovation of Beth Shean in Level VI, during which the alleged temple of Seti I was modified and gained a closed shrine among other Egyptian facets, was probably related to this historical event. The temple was then dedicated to Re-Harachte. The Horus bird of limestone *ca* 44 cm high could refer to this god venerated in the restored naos. See Zwickel, 1994, 186–191; Werning 2005, 223.

[11] Na^caman, 1977, 168–177 = Na^caman, 2005, 195–203, esp. 200–202; Ahituv, 1984, 200, stresses also its special position as a domain of the Pharaoh after its conquest by Thutmosis III.

[12] Murnane, 1990, 42-45 (though on p. 43, note 35, he apparently mixed up Helck's and Na^caman's [sic] identification); Yurco, 1986, 189–215; Staubli, 1991, 47f; 58f. I here ignore the discussion about Israel and Yano^cam in the Merenptah stela and the rediscovery of his Palestinian campaign on a relief in Karnak (Yurco and others). Elsewhere, I hope to make clear that the strong parallellism of Merenptah's and Seti I's battle reliefs strengthens the case for a northern, i.e. Syrian–Lebanese situation for Yanu^cam.

[13] See, for instance, Clauß, 1907, 34–35; Albright, 1924–25, 18–23; Redford, 1992, 181. I think that most of Albright's argument is still valid, despite the doubts expressed by Aharoni, 1947, 125ff; Aharoni, 1979, 53, 178, 443; Ahituv, 1984, 199–200, n. 620. *Pace* the identification with Tell el-Na^cam about 20 km north of Beth Shean or with nearby Tell el-Abeidiyeh (Aharoni, 1979, 53, 178, 443 and others), see Na^caman, 2005, 195–196.

[14] Kaplan, 1978, 157-169. It is striking that the site of Tell al-Na^cimeh (also Khirbet or Tell el-Na^cam, Grid Ref. 205296) was proposed for the identification of Pharaonic Yanu'am (Clauß, Albright) as for Yanoah (Kaplan).

[15] Albright and Rowe, 1928, 286-287, Plate XXIX:2.

[16] *PM* VII, 383; Kitchen, 1969 I,17.

strongly resembles the similar scene of Seti I before Re-Harachte on the larger Beth Shean stele. Its dedication to Amun-Re is no coincidence, if one realizes that the larger Beth Shean stele is devoted to Re-Harachte. The different steles must relate to the different military operations of the divisions in Seti I's army. The action of the Amun division in the Yarmūk area between Pahil (Pella) and Tell al-Shihāb brings us close to Tall Zarʿa, even more so if we identify this Hammat with el-Hammah in the lower Yarmūk Valley as others have done before us, a town just north of Umm Qays / Gadara, the Hammat Gader from later Jewish sources and the Ammatha of Byzantine and Arab tradition.[17]

8.3 In search of Tall Zarʿa in the Egyptian topography
(Fig. 8.1 and 8.2)

Though one might first search for Tall Zarʿa in the battle reliefs of Seti I on the North Wall of the Great Hypostyle in the Temple of Karnak, let me first deal with a suggestion made by H. Clauß, who long ago identified Tall Zarʿa with 'Sarki' (as he spelled Zarqu) in EA 256.[18] His suggestion to find Zarqu in Tall Zarʿa in the Wādī al-ʿArab was primarily based on the idea of a greater area of *kur*Gari and the erroneous equation with the recent name of the Jordan or Rift Valley, al-Ghor. However this would require a form *kur*Ha-ri, comparable to Hazati alongside Azati for Ghazze / Azzah / Gaza. That Zarʿa is a corruption of Sarku or Zarqu is hardly plausible and was wisely not suggested by Clauß in so many words. The team of the Scandinavian expedition at Tall al-Fukhar thinks that Tall al-Fukhar (10 km north-east of Irbid in Wādī al-Shallalah) might be the site of Amarna Zarqu. It has indeed a LB I–II level of occupation. Interestingly, it lies close to Khirbet al-Zayraqūn, which, however can hardly be LB Zarqu, though this name is promising, because it is largely an Early Bronze site.[19] Still, I think that a site north of the Yarmūk is more plausible, because the majority of the list of rebelling and conquered towns in this letter are situated in *kur*Gari that at present is often understood as a corruption of *kur*Ga-<šu>-ri, which would represent Biblical Geshur north of the Yarmūk.[20]

In the vividly illustrated battle reliefs about Seti I's first campaign to Palestine, Yanuʿam is followed by a partly

destroyed town *qa-dú-rù*.[21] More precisely the city is called *qa-dú-rù m pꜣ tꜣ n ha-an-má* 'Qaduru in the land of Hanma'. If the battle with the Shosu bedouins in Sinai and the following assault on Pi-Canaan (= Gaza?) along the Mediterranean coast be depicted in the lower scenes on the wall, then the higher band of scenes was similarly south–north orientated, *i.e.* the town between the cedar woods and Yanuʿam lies further to the north or east. Helck identified the town as the predecessor of Umm Qays / Gadara.[22] But if my interpretation of the Egyptian battle reliefs and inscriptions is correct, the place could be further north in a wooded area like Yanuʿam. Beyond this city are the submissive chiefs of the Lebanon, some felling trees for the pharaoh, perhaps cedars for the barque of Amun.[23] Perhaps, the same city is also mentioned in the lists of Ramesses II in the Luxor Temple, among a series of toponyms, of which Tahsi (Biblical Tahash, Amarna *Taḫši*) is well known.[24] If so, this implies also a locality for Yanuʿam in the Lebanon area.

In all probability, however, there is a differently spelled toponym *qa/gá-da-ra* attested in the lists of Seti I on the North Wall; in any case in one of the two versions found on either side of the entrance.[25] Analysis of these lists shows that they are composed of several groups of toponyms. The core of the lists consists of the four towns which Seti I mentioned in his first Beth Shean stele (see quotation above). In the minor lists in the Abydos Temple, they occur on the top of the lists! A separate group is the list of coastal cities, which runs from Acre to Tyre and Usu = inland Tyre.

This is in consonance with the strategy of Seti I. After seemingly the Seth division had reconquered Yanuʿam and Qaduru / Qadruru, apparently by approaching from inland Lebanon, he secured the coastal area from Acre to Tyre. In memory of these martial exploits, he also left a stele at Tyre.[26] In the light of this grouping, it seems a matter of course to surmise that the lists continue with towns in the inlands of southern Syria where the Amun division was sent. About Beth Anath scholarly opinions differ. The majority of scholars set it, however, in northern Canaan / southern Lebanon (later the highlands

---

[17] See, for instance Rowe, 1930, 25–26, Fig 4. Unfortunately, the archaeological evidence does not favour such an identification. Late Bronze and Iron Age occupation have not yet been attested at the site of Roman-Byzantine and Jewish Hammat-Gader = al-Hammah. Most scholars identify this Pharaonic Hammat with *Tell al-Hammah*, 16 km south of Beth Shean (Albright 1925–26; R. Gophna and Y. Porath, in Kochavi, 1972, 214 (no. 55); Cahill *et al.*, 1987, 1988; Ahituv, 1984, 113, although he identifies Thutmosis III's *Hamatu* (I:16a,c I:16b, V:3) with Hamath Gader on the Yarmūk River.

[18] Clauß, 1907, 51 no. 83. I thank Dieter Vieweger kindly for drawing my attention to this reference.

[19] See the summary on Zayraqūn in Negev and Gibson, 2005, 553.

[20] See Aharoni, 1979, 175 Map 11 *passim*. Another possibility might be *kur*Ga-<du>-ri, reminiscent of the name Gedur / Ğedur in later Jewish, Arabian and modern sources. See, for instance, Wetzstein's report of his visit to Sheikh Saʿad and surroundings in 1861 published in Delitzsch, 1876, 566–570. Whether a relation can be established with *qa-dú-ru* (see below) read as *gá-dú-ru* on the battle reliefs and in topographical lists remains to be seen. I will discuss this problem elsewhere in my forthcoming article about EA 256.

[21] My system of transcription of Egyptian group writing follows that of Hoch, 1994, 506–512, with some slight modifications.

[22] Helck, 1962, 202–203.

[23] *ANET*³, 254c; Kitchen, 1969- I, 13, 8–9.

[24] Ahituv, 1984, 187; see for this toponym Kitchen, 1969- II, 177 23–27, 178 1–5, if it be accepted that the rendering *qa-ad-rú-rù** is correct. It is perhaps a variant of the name. The centre of the cartouche, however, is damaged and a rendering *qa-dú-rù* also plausible. If the variant *qadruru** for *qaduru** exists, one derivation might be from רדק 'to be black', though a relationship with רטק cannot be excluded, compare the Semitic loan *qa-da-rù-tá* 'incense' (Sivan-Kochavi, 1992; 85, Hoch, 1994, 305 No. 440). Semitic toponyms with רטק are possible, see Qitron=Qata(r)t in Zebulon (Judges 1:30, Joshua 19:15). Martin Noth suggested identification with Kafr Qatra (Noth, *ABLAK 2*, 31-32; Helck, 1962, 203).

[25] Simons, 1937, 140; Kitchen, 1969 I, 29–32, and Helck, 1962, 202–203, accepted the rendering (in the form *q-d-[<w>-r]* or as *ga-da-ra*). Because the name is damaged in both lists, *qa/gá-dú-ra* instead of *qa/gá-da-ra* cannot be excluded.

[26] Unfortunately, an only partially preserved mainly rhetorical stele. See Chéhab, 1969, 32; Pl. VIII, 3; Kitchen, 1969- I, 117.

of Galilee) with Yanu^cam and Tyre forming a kind of northern border established after the first campaign.

The other toponyms as far as related to Canaan and the Levant were presumably on the other side of Lake Kinneret, closing the provisional border at Hazor from the east. Among the toponyms on the east side of Lake Kinneret, *Qarat ^cAnbu** has been identified with Tell al-Shihāb in the Yarmūk Valley. This equation of *Qarat ^cAnbu** and *^cÊnu ^cAnabi** (the *Ḥeni Anabi* of the Amarna letter EA 256:26) as the site where Seti I or more likely his Amun division set up the stele for Amun-Re has been broadly accepted, though not conclusively proven.[27] Perhaps, this town was the furthest point eastwards of this punitive expedition and the Amun division made a pincer movement from there into the direction of Hazor. This might explain why a city such as Ashtartu in the uplands of Bashan was ignored during this first campaign. This Late Bronze Pharaonic Qadara / Gádara in the region of the Yarmūk must be in some way related to the Hellenistic–Roman–Byzantine Gadara / Umm Qays. This more recent city, however, has no clear vestiges of occupation before the Hellenistic Period. Tall Zar^ca is the largest tell in the vicinity where occupational levels from the Early Bronze Age until the first part of Iron Age II are attested. It could therefore be ancient Qadara / Gadara, but a definitive identification requires more evidence. Did the inhabitants transfer the name to the new city of Gadara in Hellenistic times[28] or was there a stage with seasonal movement between the two?

8.4 Gadara in later Egyptian texts

Gadara is not mentioned anywhere else in the lists of Seti I. It does not occur on the Qurneh sphinx from the Mortuary Temple of Seti I nor in the Abydos Temple, perhaps because of the fragmentary state of these lists. From the reign of Ramesses II, there are quite a number of topographical lists but most are fragmentary and some Semitic names have been replaced by Nubian toponyms. For this investigation, these lists offer little additional information. The first series of Seti I: Pahil, Hammat, Beth Shean and Yanu^cam, together with the coastal cities and an occasional Transjordanian town (*Qarat ^cAnba*), were taken over by Ramesses II, who consolidated and even expanded the territories conquered by Seti I before and after the Battle of Qadesh (1274 BCE). Not only did he set up his own steles at Beth Shean, but he also erected some along the coastal road (Nahr el-Kalb), one at Tyre also in Lebanon and also some others in Jordan at al-

Turrah (perhaps also from the 4th year)[29] and in southern Syria, one at Qarnaim / Sheikh Sa^cad (later venerated as the "Stone of Job") and another recently discovered at Kiswe south of Damascus.[30] Other documents and inscriptions also show that the frontier was maintained as far as Yanu^cam during the 19th Dynasty and the first part of the 20th Dynasty, although Merenptah had to restore Egyptian authority in that region after a revolt in his 5th Year (Israel stele 1207 BCE).

The stela of Kiswe is not significant for its rhetorical content, but for its particular date and provenance. It is dated in the 56th Year of Ramesses II (1223 BCE). As such, it is an eloquent testimony that the area around Damascus (Upe) was still under Egyptian control about ten years before the death of Ramesses II, a situation that continued under Merenptah[31] and his successors up to Ramesses III, who had to admit that the enemy took hold of Amurru in his 8th Year (1176 BCE). He was forced to fall back on the military base at Beth Shean which was renovated by him and became the seat of the Egyptian governor.[32] But before this decline in Egyptian rule over Canaan, there is evidence that the Ramessides had still a number of other advanced bases and fortresses in the area enforcing Egyptian rule and administration, e.g. in Megiddo, Jaffa, Tyre, Yanu^cam and even in the province of Upe.

Finally, our identification of Tall Zar^ca as Gadara is perhaps also supported by a passage from the 'Satirical Letter' written by Hori to Amenemopet, a literary document dating from the beginning of the 12th Century BCE.[33] In pAnastasi I:21, 2, the author embarks on another subject describing an itinerary, which leads past Byblos, Beirut, Sidon and Sarepta, across the River Litani to Usu, i.e. inland Tyre. At Acre, he turns inland into the direction of Lake Kinneret. From what follows, it is evident that he crosses the Jordan and moves into Transjordan. After mentioning the road branching off to Hazor, he continues on his way to Hammat, either Hammat south of Beth Shean or Hammat in the Yarmūk Valley. After crossing the stream, certainly the Jordan, there is the remarkable sequence *há-má-ta da-ga-ra (det) da-ga-ar-'i-ir (det)* (usually read as Hamat, Dagan and Dagan-el). I wonder whether the strange sequence Dagan and Dagan-el contains a dittography. I suggest, therefore, a slight correction interchanging the first two groups of

---

[27] Ahituv, 1984, 127; Kitchen, 1992, 26. The town is also attested under Ramesses II (List XXIII+XXIV no 41; pAnastasi I, 22:4).

[28] Such transfers of names are well known, in particular if the new city replaced the old one at a short distance (e.g. Beth Shean), but Tall Zar^ca is situated in the valley and Gadara is *ca* 5 km to the NE on the ridge between Wādī al-^cArab and the Yarmūk Valley. An interesting example of such a wandering toponym over a larger distance is Late Bronze–Early Hellenistic Paphos on Cyprus. It became Palaipaphos after foundation of the new harbour town Nea Paphos, 15 km to the west of ancient Paphos and now known as Paphos instead of the ancient centre of the Paphian Kingdom. Another question still to be answered is, how this name of Gadar(a) was kept alive during the occupational gap of four centuries from Iron II to Hellenistic times.

[29] See note 2.
[30] Yoyotte, 1999, 44–58.
[31] pAnastasi III 1, 9-10; 7,10-11 mentions a certain Amen-em-opet as royal overseer in the foreign lands from Tjaru to Upe. Further, there is a town called 'Town of Merenptah Hotep-Maat-Re in the land of Aram' where an overseer of the stables, Pa-Mer-Khetem, son of Ani was staying (pAnastasi III 5, 4ff), but who returned carrying letters from a commander Pa-Re-em-heb (*ANET*[3], 258-9). One may surmise that this town is the town called 'Ramesses-Meri-Amun in Upe' in the diplomatic correspondence of Ramesses II with the Hittite Court.
[32] Zie *ANET*[3], 262; Dijkstra, 2003, 198. If the title "Lord of the Jubilee" found on one of de limestone doorposts at Beth Shean applies to Ramesses III, Egyptian rule of northern Canaan may have lasted even until the second part of the 12th Century BCE.
[33] Fischer-Elfert, 1986; other translations *ANET*[3], 475–479; *COS* 3, 9–14, Wente, 1990, 98–110.

da-ga-ra to give the sequence *há-má-ta ga!-da!-ra.*[34] That name is remarkably similar to Hammat-Gader from the Rabbinical, early Christian and Arabic sources, which distinguish this Hammat from other places of that name. But even if we read here two separate names, it is probable that Hammat on the Yarmūk is meant, followed by nearby Gadara and the still unknown town of Dagan-el, as the author calls it, the parade ground of every *mahir* (kind of soldier), suggesting that we deal here with an important military approach.

8.5 Conclusion

Though the author of the Satirical Letter mentioned a road branching off to Hazor, he continued along the road to Syria, crossing the River Jordan below Lake Kinneret east of Beth Shean and turned northwards into Syria from there. This author seems to be familiar with an important road passing Tall Zarʿa / Gadara (or perhaps Hammat Gadara) and further east along al-Turrah bending north, crossing the Yarmūk at Tell al-Shihāb towards the area north of the Yarmūk, which he describes in the next paragraph (22.2). If so, Gadara, which appears for the first time in the reign of Seti I (*ca* 1293 BCE), is attested until the beginning of the Early Iron Age. The town at the site of Tall Zarʿa in the Late Bronze and Early Iron Age is most probably the 2nd Millennium Gadara and predecessor of Hellenistic and Roman-Byzantine Gadara / Umm Qays.

---

[34] Albright, 1924-25, 22 and Naʿaman, 2005, 198 had suspected a corruption of Gadara to *dgr*.

FIG. 8.1 MAP: TOPONYMS AND IDENTIFICATIONS.

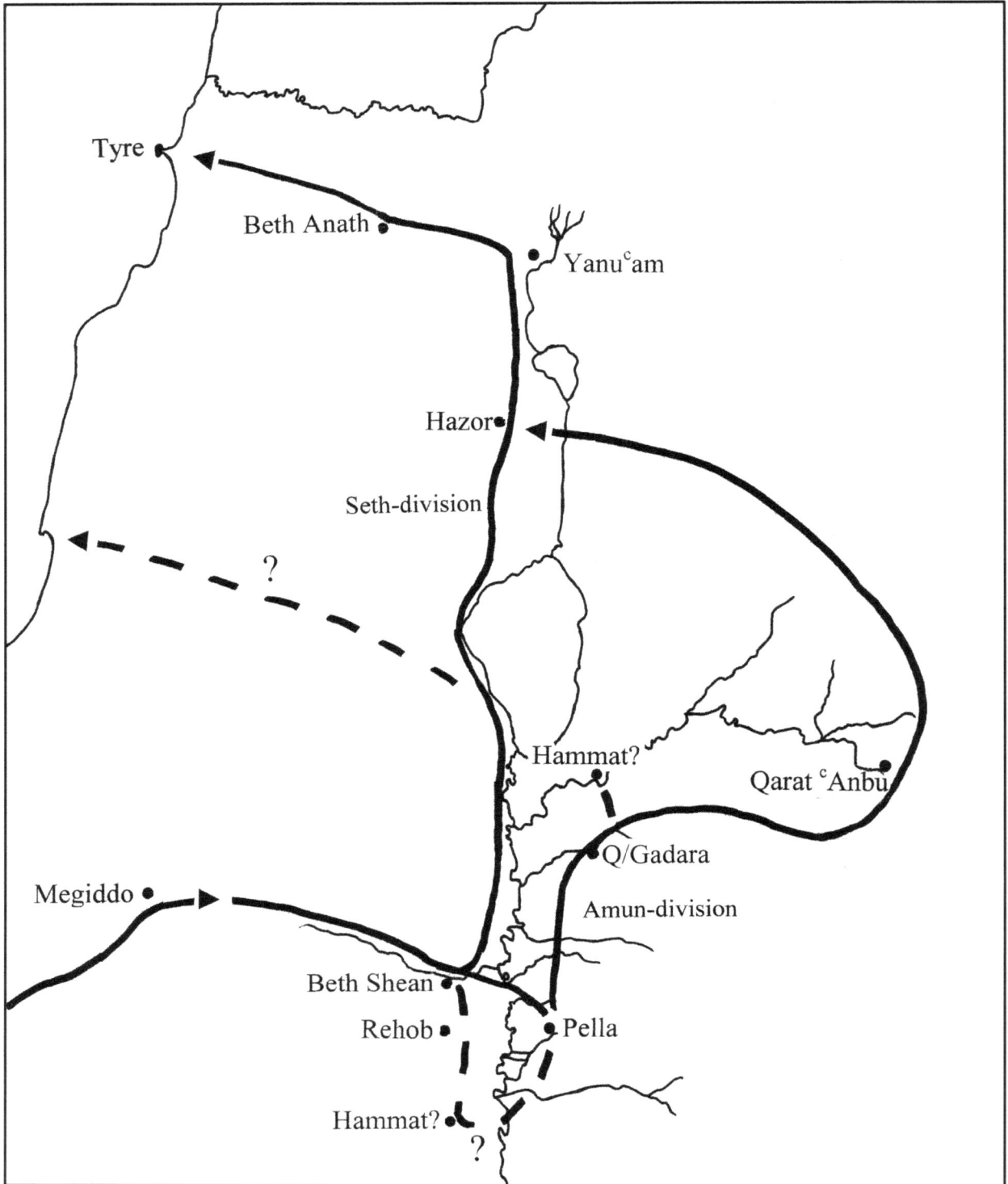

FIG. 8.2 MAP: MILITARY CAMPAIGN IN THE FIRST YEAR OF SETI I.

CHAPTER 9

CONCLUSIONS

The sondage of 2001–2002 probed the upper strata of the tell on the west side of the platform and penetrated deep enough to touch the deposit of yellowish loamy soil, which we suppose to date from the Late Bronze Age. Although this deposit was not excavated, we thought the hypothesis of its date was justified by the date of Stratum IV (see below), by the proportion of (Middle Bronze IIC–)Late Bronze I–II finds mixed in with the contents of Stratum IV[1] and by the difference in building materials and architecture of Phase V.2, from the strata above. On this loamy deposit there are two solid strata from the Iron Age, one from the Late Roman–Early Byzantine and one from the Early Islamic periods.

The sequence of periods of settlement and intervals between encountered in the sondage may need modification when larger areas of the tell are investigated,[2] but in general we found confirmation for our hypotheses in the preliminary data published by the joint teams of the Biblisch Archäologisches Institut, Wuppertal, and the German Protestant Institute, Amman.[3]

The sequence from the Late Bronze building remains (Wall W19–W19a) to the Iron Age I Stratum IV floors was characterized by elements of discontinuity and of continuity. Although there were no traces of a violent end to the buildings of the Late Bronze period, the thick loamy deposit may be interpreted as the remains of a gradual decay of mud-brick buildings, a period in which the area lay waste. The interval between this deposit and the Floors Fl.K–Fl.H and the Walls W18–W13 is represented by disturbances of the large Pits P2–P3 and by the E–W Wall W20. However most of the ceramic finds in Stratum IV belong to pottery types dated to the Late Bronze II-Iron Age I period[4] and they were evidence of a certain cultural continuity on the site, which has also been documented elsewhere in northern Jordan.[5]

The charcoal sample from the most recent floor of Stratum IV, Floor Fl.H in Phase IV.2, was dated to 13th-12th cent. BCE[6] by carbon-14 analysis, which to a certain

extent overlapped with the carbon-14 date of the 12th - 11th cent. BCE[7] of a charcoal sample from Pit P2a, into which parts of Floor Fl.H were assumed to have slid away. So, based on these analyses the end of settlement of Stratum IV may be dated to the 11th Century BCE as datum a quo. This stratum, however, is characterized by the ceramic repertoire of Iron Age I, which in the current debate is estimated to end in the early 10th century BCE.[8] As in the next strata only a few Iron IIA sherds are found, we consider the first half of the 10th century as a date for the end of the Stratum IV-settlement (Phase IV.2).

After this settlement of Stratum IV, an interval commenced, with evidence of discontinuity: a deposit of soil on Floor Fl.H, then a thick layer of ash, upon which another deposit of soil (Phases IV.1, III.3) before settlement recommenced in Phase III.2.[9] We dated this last Iron Age settlement to Iron Age IIB (9th–8th Century BCE), because of the finds of Iron IIA–B pottery in the deposits of the interval.[10] Therefore this interval is to be dated between the first half of the 10th and the 9th Century BCE, a dating which corresponds with the situation documented elsewhere in northern Jordan.[11] The thick layer of ash in the deposits of the interval may point to a natural or military catastrophe, here or nearby on the tell.[12]

In general Stratum III was followed by a long interval of non-settlement starting with Iron IIC, which was recorded also elsewhere in northern Jordan.[13] Sporadic finds of Iron IIB–C pottery[14] in the reddish soil between Phase III.1 and Strata II–I indicated that there may have been some activity elsewhere on the tell after Iron IIB, which corresponds to Iron IIC presence on some other sites in northern Jordan.[15] In the sondage area, this interval lasted until the Late Roman period (3rd–early 4th century CE).

---

[1] Fig. 4.8: 2, 4, 6–7, 10, 14, 17–19, 21–28.
[2] Vieweger 2002, 164, 172–173. The data from the survey 2001 showed that the finds from the various periods were not evenly distributed over the tell.
[3] Vieweger and Häser, 2005, 2007a, 2007b.
[4] For Late Bronze II–Iron I pottery, see Fig. 4.4:1–8, 10, 13-15, 17–21, 24; 4.5:1–12, 14–15; 4.6:1, 4–9; 4.7:1, 3–5, 8–9, 11; 4.8:2, 5, 16, 20.
[5] Herr and Najjar, 2001, 323–328; Ji, 1995, 122–126, 131–132, 138; Lenzen et al., 1985, 152-155; Lenzen and McQuitty, 1988, 268; Strange, 1997, 402-403; Lamprichs, 2007, 197-198,277-279, 302.
[6] Chapt.2.5, footnote 9. UtC no. 15085: 14C Age [BP] 2983 ±50; Calender Age [cal BP] 3077-3243 = 1127-1293 BCE (97% probability).

[7] Chapt.2.5, footnote 15. UtC no. 15084: 14C Age [BP] 2920 ±50; Calender Age [cal BP] 2991-3160 = 1041-1210 BCE (97% probability). The slightly younger date of this sample may reflect the fact that the upper fill of Pit P2 may have some post-Phase IV.2 elements mixed in.
[8] Mazar, 2008, 98-99; Bruins, van der Plicht and Mazar, 2003, 318;. However, for a discussion on the "High" and "Low Chronology"-dates of the Iron Age II-period, see Finkelstein and Piasetzky, 2007, 248, 256-257; Gilboa and Sharon, 2008, 152.
[9] Fig. 4.3: 7,16; 4.7:7.
[10] Fig. 4.3.1,5,10. From this deposit. there is an incidental intrusion of Iron IIA–B in the top of the P2a fill (Fig. 4.3:12).
[11] Ji, 1995, 123–126, 131–132, 138.
[12] Cf. Vieweger and Häser, 2007b, 159, 163.
[13] Herr and Najjar, 2001, 334–335.
[14] Fig. 4.3.2, 13, 18.
[15] Mare, 1984, 40; Strange, 1997, 402-403; Lamprichs, 2007, 198-200,283-285,297-300,303-304.

The Iron Age pottery repertoire originated mainly from the Iron Age I–IIB periods and was composed of ordinary household pottery types (cooking pots, craters, bowls, shallow bowls, pithoi, jars and jugs) and hardly any luxury ceramics or lamps. An exception was the painted jar with a motive of antithetic snakes (reconstruction in Fig. 4.3.19), reminiscent of the snakes on a cult stand from Beth Shean[16] and the black-and-red painted Late Bronze jar excavated on Tall Zar[c]a by the joint team of the BAI Wuppertal and the German Protestant Institute, Amman.[17]

Counts of sherds produce a survey of proportions of pottery classes within a repertoire. The results may, however, depend on whether only rim sherds or also profiled diagnostic sherds are included in the counts. Therefore an other method of estimation may be preferred, by which for the various ceramic types the relationship between rim length and pot surface area is calculated and body sherds are considered in the counts as well. Such a method may effectuate a fine tuning of the proportions of pottery classes and a better analysis of the complexity of the ceramic repertoire in an early stage of processing the finds.

The areas of the Iron Age and the Late Roman–Early Byzantine period excavated in the sondage functioned as areas of food preparation, as may be concluded from the many household ceramics and stone utensils, like millstones, pestles and mortars. The stone utensils are all made of basalt, which may have been quarried near Umm Qays or around Lake Kinneret and on the Golan.

In Chapter 8, we considered Tall Zar[c]a in its historical context. The tell lay on one of the main commercial and military roads inland into Jordan and Syria.[18] Because the tell was occupied by a fortified city in the Late Bronze Period, which was in decline at the end of the period and which was resettled in the Early Iron Age, first by an open settlement and later in Iron Age II again by a fortified settlement,[19] a search for its identity in historical sources is warranted. Analysis of Egyptian topographical lists and historical accounts and literature of the New Kingdom contained evidence of a city called Qadara / Gadara in the military, administrative and commercial road system in the Late Bronze and Early Iron Age. It is plausible to assume that this Gadara was the predecessor of Hellenistic–Roman Gadara. Tall Zar[c]a is not only the largest settlement in the immediate region of Umm Qays–Gadara, but shares with the latter its orientation towards Beth Shean. Identification of Tall Zar[c]a with 'old Gadara' is therefore probable.

This identification does not imply that this city was an Egyptian stronghold or a garrison city like Beth Shean.

As yet, few *aegyptica* have been discovered on the tell. A turquoise bead (Fig. 5.4), a few scarabs and a fragment of faience ware[20] hardly imply an official Egyptian presence. Changes in the settlement pattern in the Iron Age are as yet difficult to grasp and to explain historically. The repertoire of household ceramics continues Late Bronze types and traditional skills of production into the Early Iron Period. There were no obvious differences in social standing from similar settlements and settlers in southern Syria, Galilee and the Cis-Jordan hill-country. Somewhere in the beginning of Iron Age IIA, the house in our area was abandoned (in the first half of the 10th cent. BCE?) and rebuilding did not start before another calamity or military attack had happened, as shown by a thick layer of ash that lay on another reddish deposit (Fig. 2.17-2.19; 2.21; 2.36; Phases IV.1–III.3). The interval in settlement was perhaps associated with the advance of Aramean tribes into Israelite Gilead. If not an earthquake, the agent of destruction could have been the campaign of Ben Hadad ben Tabrimmon *ca* 883 BCE (1 Kings 15:20), which left also other cities damaged and destroyed.[21] There is a rather general consensus that cities in northern Transjordan, like those of southern Syria and Galilee were depopulated and ceased to exist after the campaigns of Tiglath-Pileser III (734–732) against Israel and 'Damascus' / Damaśeq (2 Kings 15:29).[22] Perhaps also Tall Zar[c]a = Gadara fell victim to these massive deportations as did other places in northern Jordan.[23] Because the last Iron Age house (Phase III.2) did not exist for longer than a century (Chap. 2.4), it was perhaps part of a resettlement of Gilead during the reign of King Jehoahaz or Jehoash of Israel, restoring an Israelite presence in the area *ca* 810 BCE (2 Kings 13:5, 22–25).[24]

---

[16] *NEAEHL* I, 222.

[17] Vieweger and Häser, 2007b, 155.

[18] Vieweger and Häser, 2005, 2007b; Dijkstra *et al.* 2005a,b.

[19] Vieweger and Häser, 2007a, 10-13; idem 2007b, 159. In the sondage the outer western wall of the latest Iron Age II, settlement was not found or excavated because we did not probe the area below the track of Wall z (Chap. 2.2; Fig. 2.7; 2.16-17;2.19).

[20] Vieweger and Häser, 2007b, 157–159.

[21] Ji, 1995, 136; Bruins, van der Plicht, Mazar, 2003, 316–317.

[22] See for a different view based on the finds at Tall Juhfiyah, Lamprichs, 2007, 283-285, 298-299, 303-304.

[23] Herr and Najjar, 2001, 334–335.

[24] Donner, in Hayes & Miller, 1977, 1990[3], 413–414; Veenhof, 2001, 241.

Table 9.1 Chart: Stratigraphy and chronology

Strat./Phase	Period	Date	Description	Architecture etc.
V.2	LB IIB?	1300-1200 BCE	End LB settlement; Interval?	W19-W19a; loam deposit
V.1; IV.5,P2b	Iron IA	1200-1150 BCE	Settlement?	W20; lower fill Pit P2 and P3
IV.4-2 (IV.5)	Iron IA/B-early IIA	1150-early 10th cent. BCE	Settlement	W13, W14, W15, W16, W17, W18; Fl.H, Fl.I, Fl.J, Fl.K: floors with traces of cooking activities (upper fill Pit P2 and P3)
IV.1-III.3	Iron IIA-B	early 10th-mid 9th cent. BCE	Interval: no settlement; advance of Arameans?	deposit, ash layer, deposit
III.2-1	Iron IIB	mid 9th cent.-732 BCE	Settlement	W10, W11, W12; Fl.E, Fl.F, Fl.G; M1
III.1?	Iron IIC	7th-6th cent. BCE	Interval: settlement elswhere?; deportation by Assyrians?	Few sherds; thick deposit
	Persian-Roman	5th cent. BCE-2nd cent. CE	Interval: no settlement	
II.2-1	Late Roman-Early Byzantine	3rd-4th cent. CE	settlement	W7, W8,W9; Fl.C, Fl.D
	Byzantine	4^{e}-7^{e} cent. CE	Interval: settlement elswhere?	sherds
I.4-2	Omayyad	7th-8th cent. CE	Settlement	W1, W2, W4, W5, W6; Fl.A, Fl.B
	Abbasid-Ayyubid	8^{e}-12^{e} nC	Interval: no settlement	
I.1	Mamluk	13th-15th cent. CE	Settlement?	Pit P1

ABLAK	- M.Noth, *Aufsätze zur biblischen Landes- und Altertumskunde 1-2*, Neukirchen-Vluyn 1971.
ADPV	- *Abhandlungen des Deutschen Palästina-Vereins*, Wiesbaden.
ADAJ	- *Annual of the Department of Antiquities of Jordan*, Amman.
AASOR	- *Annual of the American Schools of Oriental Research*, New Haven.
ANET³	- *J.B. Pritchard (ed), Ancient Near Eastern Texts Relating to the Old Testament, Third Edition with supplement*, Princeton New Jersey 1969
AOAT	- *Altes Orient und Altes Testament*, Münster.
ÄuL	- *Ägypten und Levante*, Wien.
BA	- *Biblical Archaeologist*, Boston.
BAH	- *Bibliothéque Archéologique et Historique*, Beyrouth.
BAR	*Britisch Archaelogical Reports IntS*, Oxford
BASOR	- *Bulletin of the American School of Oriental Research*, New Haven.
BMB	- *Bulletin du Musée de Beyrouth*
BRL²	- *K.Galling (ed), Biblisches Reallexicon (Handbuch zum Alten Testament. Erste Reihe 1),2., neugestaltete Auflage*, Tübingen 1977
BSFE	- *Bulletin de la Société française d'égyptologie*,
COS	- *The Context of Scripture*, Leyden.
EA	- J.A. Knudtzon, *Die El-Amarna Tafeln* (VAB 2*); EA 1-358;* A. Rainey, *El-Amarna Tablets 359-379 (AOAT* 8).
IEJ	- *Israel Exploration Journal*, Jerusalem.
JADIS	- G. Palumbo (ed.), *Jordanian Antiquities Database and Information System*, Amman 1994.
JARCE	- *Journal of the American Research Center in Egypt*, Cairo.
JEA	- *Journal of Agyptian Archaeology*, London.
NEA	- *Near Eastern Archaeology*, Boston.
NEAEHL	- E. Stern (ed), *The New Encyclopedia of Archaeological Excavations in the Holy Land, I-V*, Jerusalem, 1993-2008.
OBO	- *Orbis Biblicus et Orientalis*, Freiburg Schweiz, Göttingen
PÄ	- *Probleme der Ägyptologie* - Leiden
PEQ	- *Palestine Exploration Quarterly*, London.
PM	- *Porter & Moss, Topographical Bibliography*, Oxford.
PSBF	- *Publications of the Studium Biblicum Franciscanum*, Jerusalem.

SHAJ	- *Studies in the History and Archaeology of Jordan*, Amman.
TUAT	- *Texte aus der Umwelt des Alten Testaments*,Gütersloh.
UF	- *Ugarit Forschungen*, Münster.
ZDPV	- *Zeitschrift des Deutschen Palästina-Vereins*, Wiesbaden.

Adan-Bayewitz, A.
1993   *Common Pottery in Roman Galilee. A Study of Local Trade*, Ramat Gan.

Aharoni, Y.
1947   *The Settlement of the Israelite Tribes in Upper Galilee*, Jerusalem (Hebrew).

Aharoni, Y.
1979   *The Land of the Bible. A Historical Geography*, Second, revised edition, London.

Ahituv, S.
1984   *Canaanite Toponyms in ancient Egyptian Documents*, Leyden.

Albright, W.F.
1925   'Bronze Age Mounds of Northern Palestine and Hauran,' *BASOR* 19, 5–19.

Albright, W.F.
1924-25 'The Jordan Valley in the Bronze Age,' *AASOR* 6, 13–74.

Albright, W.F. and A. Rowe
1928   'A Royal Stele of the New Empire from Galilee', *JEA* 14 (1928) 286-287.

Aldred, C.
1978   *Jewels of the Pharaohs*, London.

Amiran, R.
1956   'The Millstone and the Potter's wheel,' *Eretz Israel* 4 , 46–49 (Hebr).

Amiran, R.
1969   *Ancient Pottery of the Holy Land*, Jerusalem.

Åström, P.
1972   *The Swedish Cyprus Expedition, Vol. IV, part 1c. The Late Cypriote Bronze Age. Architecture and Pottery*, Lund.

Beck, C.W. *et al.*
2004   'The uses of Cypriote White-Slip Ware inferred from organic residue analysis,' *ÄuL* 14. 13-19.

Beit-Arieh, I.
1985   'Serabit el-Khadim: New Metalurgical and chronological Aspects,' *Levant* 17, 89-116.

Bloch Smith E. and B.A. Nakhai
1999   'A Landscape comes to live: The Iron Age I,' *NEA* 62, 62–92.

Briend, J. and J.-B. Humbert
1980   *Tell Keisan (1971-1976) une cite phénicienne en Galilée* (Orbis Biblicus et Orientalis, Ser. Arch. 1), Fribourg-Göttingen-Paris.

Bruins, H.J., J. van der Plicht and A. Mazar
2003 '¹⁴C Dates from Tel Rehov: Iron-Age Chronology, Pharaohs, and Hebrew Kings,' *Science* 300, 315-318.

Cahill, J., G.Lipton and D. Tarler
1987 'Tell el-Hammah, 1987,' *IEJ* 37, 280-283.

Cahill, J., G.Lipton and D. Tarler
1988 'Tell el-Hammah, 1988,' *IEJ* 38, 191-194.

Chambon, A.
1984 *Tell el-Far'ah 1. L'Age du Fer* (Éditions Recherche sur les Civilisations, mémoire 31), Paris.

Chéhab, M.
1969 'Noms de personnalités égyptiennes découverts au Liban,'*BMB* 22 (1969) 1-47.

Clauß, H.
1907 'Die Städte der El-Amarnabriefe und die Bibel,' *ZDPV* 30, 1–79.

Crowfoot, J.W., G.M. Crowfoot and K.M. Kenyon
1957 *Samaria-Sebaste III. The Objects*, London.

Dalman, G.
1935 *Arbeit und Sitte in Palästina* IV, Bertelsmann, Gütersloh.

Dajani, R.W.
1970 'A Late Bronze – Iron Age Tomb Excavated at Sahab, 1968,' *ADAJ* 15, 29-64.

Delitzsch, F.
1876 *Das Buch Iob*, (BCAT VI/2), Leipzig.

Dever W.G. *et al.*
1986 *Gezer IV: The 1969–71 Seasons in Field VI, the "Acropolis"* The Hebrew Union College Jerusalem.

Dijkstra, M.
2003 'Ugarit en Egypte: een moeizame relatie,' in: R.J. Demarée and K.R.Veenhof, Zij schreven geschiedenis. Historische documenten uit het Oude Nabije Oosten (2500-100 v.Chr.), (Mededelingen en verhandelingen van het Vooraziatisch-Egyptisch Genootschap „Ex Oriente Lux" XXXIII), Leiden-Leuven, 190-199.

Dijkstra, J., M. Dijkstra, D. Vieweger and K. Vriezen
2005a 'Regionaal archeologisch onderzoek nabij *Umm Qes* (ant. Gadara): de opgravingen op *Tell Zera'a* en de ligging van Laatbrons Gadara,' *Phoenix* 51, 5-26.

Dijkstra, J., M. Dijkstra and K.J.H. Vriezen
2005b 'The Gadara-Region-Project: Preliminary Report of the Sondage on Tall Zarᶜa (2001-2002) and the Identification of Late Bronze Age Gadara', *ADAJ* 49 (2005), 177-188.

Dijkstra, M.
2009 'The 'hind of the dawn': on a seal-impression from Tall Zar'a (Jordan),' (forthcoming).

Donelly, P.
2004 'Chocolate-on-White Ware: Tomb and Tall Vessel Typology at Pella,' in: *Studies in the History and Archeaology of Jordan* VIII, Amman, 97-108.

Dornemann R.H.
1983 *The Archeology of the Transjordan in the Bronze and Iron Ages,* Milwaukee.

Dussart, O.
1998 *Le verre en Jordanie et en Syrie du Sud* (*BAH*, 152), Beyrouth.

Ebeling J.R. and Y.M. Rowan
2004 'The Archeology of the daily grind. Tools and Food Production in the southern Levant,' *NEA* 67, 108–117.

Finkelstein, I.
1988 *The Archaeology of Israelite Settlement*, Jerusalem.

Finkelstein, I.
1996 'Ethnicity and Origin of the Iron I Settlers in the Highlands of Canaan. Can the Real Israel Stand up?,' *BA* 59, 198-212.

Finkelstein, I. and E. Piasetzky
2007 'Radiocarbon Dating and the Late-Iron I in Northern Canaan,' *UF* 39, 247-260.

Fischer-Elfert H.W.
1986 *Die Satirische Streitschrift des Papyrus Anastasi I. Übersetzung und Kommentar* (Ägyptologische Abhandlungen 44) Wiesbaden .

Fischer, P.M.
1993 'Tell Abu al-Kharaz. The Swedish Jordan Expedition 1991. Second Season preliminary excavation report,' *ADAJ* 37, 279-305.

Fischer, P.M.
1997 *A Late Bronze to Early Iron Age Tomb at Sahem, Jordan* (*ADPV* 21), Wiesbaden.

Fischer P.M.
1999 'Chocolate-on-White Ware: Typology, Chronology, and Provenance: The Evidence from Tell Abu al-Kharaz, Jordan Valley,' *BASOR* 313, 1-29.

Fischer P.M.
2003 'Chocolate-on-White Ware: Further Observations and Radiocarbon Dates,' *ÄuL* 13, 51-68.

Fischer, P.M.
2006 *Tell Abu al-Kharaz in the Jordan Valley. Vol. II. The Middle and the Late Bronze Ages* (Österreichische Akademie der Wissenschaften, Denkschriften, 39), Vienna.

Fortin. M. (Ed.)
1999 *Syria, Land of Civilizations, Exhibition Catalogue Musée de la civilisation de Quebec.*

Franken, H.J.
1974 *In Search of the Jericho Potters*, (North-Holland Ceramic Studies in Archeology 1), Amsterdam–Oxford-New York.

Franken, H.J.
1992 *Excavations at Tell Deir 'Alla. The Late Bronze Age Sanctuary*, Louvain.

Franken, H.J.
1993/94 'Notes on the Typology of Pot Handles and Grips,' *Newsletter Department of Pottery Technology* 11/12, Leyden, 47-53.

Franken, H.J. and J. Kalsbeek
1969 *Excavations at Tell Deir 'Allā. I. A Stratigraphical an Analytical Study of the Early Iron Age Pottery*, Leiden.

Franken, H.J. and J. Kalsbeek
1975   *Potters of a Medieval Village in the Jordan Valley*, (North Holland Ceramic Studies in Archeology 3), Amsterdam-Oxford-New York.

Franken, H.J. and M.L. Steiner
1990   *Excavations in Jerusalem 1961-1967. Vol. II. The Iron Age Extramural Quarter on the South-East Hill*, Oxford.

Fritz, V. and A. Kempinski
1983   *Ergebnisse der Ausgrabungen auf der Hirbet el-Mšaš (Tēl Māśōś) 1972-1975* (ADPV), Harrassowitz, Wiesbaden.

Gardiner, M. and A. McQuitty
1987   'Water mills in the Wadi Arab, Jordan,' *PEQ* 119, 24-32.

Gilboa, A. and I. Sharon
2003   'An archaeological contribution to the Early Iron Age chronological debate: Alternative Chronologies for Phoenicia and their effects on the Levant, Cyprus and Greece,' *BASOR* 332, 7-80.

Gilboa, A. and I. Sharon
2008   'Between the Carmel and the Sea. Tel Dor's Iron Age Reconsidered,' *NEA* 71, 146-170.

Gitin, S.
1990   *Gezer III. A Ceramic Typology of the Late Iron II, Persian and Hellenistic Periods at Tell Gezer. Text/Data Base and Plates* (Nelson Glueck School of Biblical Archaeoloy, 8), Hebrew Union College, Jerusalem.

Glueck, N.
1951   *Explorations in Eastern Palestine IV* (AASOR 25-28), AASOR, New Haven.

Gonen, R.
1975   *Weapons of the Ancient World*, London.

Gunneweg, J., I. Perlman and J. Yellin
1983   *The Provenience, typology and chronology of eastern terra sigillata* (Qedem 17), Jerusalem.

Hanbury-Tenison, J.W.
1984   'Wadi Arab Survey 1983,' *ADAJ* 28, 385-424, 494-496.

Hardin, J.
2004   'Understanding Domestic Space: An Example from Iron Age Tel Halif,' *NEA* 67, 71-83.

Harrison, T.P. *et al.*
2004   *Megiddo 3 : final report of the stratum VI excavations*, Chicago.

Hasel, M.G.
1998   *Domination and Resistance. Egyptian Military Activity in the Southern Levant, ca 1300-1185 B.C.,* (PÄ 11), Leiden, Boston, Köln.

Häser J. and D. Vieweger
2005   'Preliminary Report on the archaelogical investigations of the Wādī al-'Arab and Tall Zar'a 2003 and 2004,' *ADAJ* 49, 135-146.

Hayes, J.H. and J.M. Miller (eds)
1990   *Israelite and Judaean History*, third impression London, Philadelphia.

Hayes, J.W.
1972   *Late Roman Pottery*, London.

Helck, W.
1962   *Die Beziehungen Ägyptens zu Vorderasien im 3. und 2. Jahrtausend v. Chr.* (Ägyptologische Abhandlungen 5), Wiesbaden.

Hennessy, J.B.
1985   'Chocolate on White Ware in Pella,' in: J. Tubb (ed.), *Palestine in the Bronze and Iron Ages: Papers in Honor of Olga Tufnell*, London, 100-113.

Herr, L.G.
2001   'The History of the Collared Pithos at Tell el-'Umeiri, Jordan,' in: S.Wolff (ed), *The Douglas L. Esse Memorial Volume*, Chicago.

Herr, L.G. and M. Najjar
2001   'The Iron Age,' in: B. MacDonald, R. Adams and P. Bienkowski (eds.), *The Archaeology of Jordan,*Academic Press, Sheffield, 323-345.

Herr, L.G., L.T. Geraty, Ø.S. LaBianca & R.W. Younker
1991   'Madeba Plains Project: The 1989 Excavations at Tell el-'Umeiri and Vicinity,' *ADA.J* 35, 155-166.

Hirschfeld, Y.
1995   *The Palestinian Dwelling in the Roman-Byzantine Period.* (PSBF, Coll. Minor 34), Franciscan Press, Jerusalem.

Hirschfeld, Y. (ed.)
1997   *The Roman Baths of Hammat Gader*, Jerusalem.

Hoch J.E.
1994   *Semitic Words in Egyptian Texts of the New Kingdom and the Third Intermediate Period*, Princeton. New Yersey.

Holland, T.A.
1977   'A Study of Palestinian Iron Age Baked Clay Figurines, with special reference to Jerusalem: Cave 1,' *Levant* 9, 121-155.

Ibrahim, M.M.
1976   'Second Season of Excavations at Sahab,' *ADAJ* 20, 55-82.

Ibrahim, M.M.
1977   'The Collared-Rim Jar of the Early Iron Age*,' in: R. Moorey and P.J. Parr (eds), *Archaeology of the Levant*, (Fs Kathleen Kenyon), London, 116-126.

Isings, C.
1957   *Roman glass from dated finds*, Groningen-Djakarta.

James F.W and P.E. McGovern
1993   *The Late Bronze Egyptian Garrison at Beth Shean: A Study of Levels VII and VIII*, Philadelphia.

Ji. C.C.
1995   'Iron Age I in Central and Northern Transjordan: an interim summary of archaeological data,' *PEQ* 127, 122-140.

Kaplan, J.
1978   'The Identification of Abel-Beth-Maachah and Janoah,' *IEJ* 28, 157–169.

Kellermann, D.
1977   'Mühle,' *BRL²*, 232–233.

Kerestes, T.M., J.M. Lundquist, B.G.Wood and K. Yassine
1978 'An Archaeological Survey of Three Reservoir Areas in Northern Jordan, 1978,' *ADAJ* 22 , 108-135.

King P.J. & L.E.Stager,
2001 *Life in Biblical Israel*, Louisville-London.

Kitchen K.A. (ed)
1969– *Ramesside Inscriptions*, 7 vols, London.

Kitchen, K.A.
1992 'The Egyptian Evidence on Ancient Jordan,' in: P. Bienkowski, *Early Edom and Moab. The Beginning of the Iron Age in Southern Jordan*, (Sheffield Archeaological Monographs 7), Sheffield, 21-34.

Kitchen, K.A.
2000 'First Beth-Shan Stela, Year 1 (2.4B),' COS II, 25-26.

Kochavi, M. (ed),
1972 *Judaea Samaria and the Golan, Archaeological Survey 1967-1968*, Jerusalem.

LaGro, H.E.
2002 *An insight into Ayyubid-Mamluk pottery. Description and analysis of a corpus of mediaeval pottery from the cane sugar production and village occupation at Tell Abu Sarbut in Jordan*, Leiden (PhD-thesis).

Lamprichs, R.W.
2007 *Tell Johfiyeh: ein archäologischer Fundplatz und seine Umgebung in Nordjordanien* (*AOAT* 344), Münster.

Lenzen, C.J. , R.L. Gordon and A.M. McQuitty
1985 'Excavations at Tell Irbid and Beit Ras, 1985,' *ADAJ* 29, 151-159.

Lenzen, C.J. and A.M. McQuitty
1988 'The 1984 survey of the Irbid/Beit Ras region,' *ADAJ* 32, 265-274.

Loffreda, S.
1974 *Cafarnao.*II *La Ceramica*, (PSBF 19), Jerusalem.

Mare, W.H.
1984 'The 1982 season at Abila of the Decapolis,' *ADAJ* 28, 39-54.

Mazar, A.
1992 *Archaeology of the Land of the Bible. 10,000-586 BCE*, (The Anchor Bible Reference Library), New York.

Mazar, A.
2008 'From 1200 to 850 B.C.E. – Remarks on Some Selected Archaeological Issues,' in: L.L. Grabbe (ed.), *Israel in Transition: from late Bronze II to Iron IIa (c. 1250-850 BCE)*, London.

McGovern, P.
1986 *The Late Bronze and Early Iron Ages of Central Transjordan: The Baq'ah Valley Project 1977-1981*, Philadelphia.

McNicoll, A.W., R.H. Smith and J.B. Hennessy
1982 *Pella in Jordan 1. An interim report on the joint University of Sydney and The College of Wooster Excavations at Pella 1979-1981*, Canberra 1982.

McNicoll, A.W., P.C. Edwards, J. Hanbury-Tenison, J.B. Hennessy, T.F. Potts, R.H. Smith, A. Walmsley and P. Watson
1992 *Pella in Jordan 2. The second interim report of the joint University of Sydney and College of Wooster Excavations at Pella 1982-1985*, (Mediterranean Archaeology Suppl. 2) Sydney.

McQuitty, A.
1984 'An Ethnographic and Archaeological Study of Clay Ovens in Jordan,' *ADAJ* 28, 259-267.

McQuitty, A.
1993 'Ovens in town and country,' *Berythus* 41, 53-76.

McQuitty, A.
1995 'Water-Mills in Jordan: Technology, Typology, Dating and Development,' *SHAJ* V, 745-751.

Mittmann, S.
1970 *Beiträge zur Siedlungs- und Territorial-geschichte des nördlichen Ostjordanlandes*, (*ADPV*), Wiesbaden.

Moritz, L.A.
1956 *Grain-Mills and Flour in Antiquity*, Clarendon Oxford.

Mulder-Hijmans, N.
2008 'The bread ovens of Tell Abu Sarbut,' in: M.L. Steiner and E.J. van der Steen (eds.), *Sacred and Sweet. Studies on the Material Culture of Tell Deir 'Alla and Tell Abu Sarbut*, (Ancient Near Eastern Studies, suppl.24), Louvain, 211-230.

Murnane W.J.
1990 *The Road to Kadesh. A Historical Interpretation of the Battle Relief of King Seti I at Karnak*, (Studies in Ancient Oriental Civilization, 42), Second Edition Revised, Chicago.

Na'aman, N.
1977 'Yeno'am,' *Tel Aviv* 4 (1977) 168–177 = Canaan in the Second Millennium B.C.E. Collected Essays Volume 2, Winowa Lake, Eisenbrauns 2005, 195–203.

Negev, A. and Sh. Gibson
2003 *Archaeological Encyclopedia of the Holy Land*, Sheffield.

Netzer, E.
1992 'Domestic Architecture in the Iron Age,' in: A. Kempinski and R. Reich (eds.), *The Architecture of Ancient Israel From the Prehistoric to the Persian Periods*, Israel Exploration Society/Jerusalem.

Petit, L.
1999 'Grinding Implements and Material found at Tall Dayr 'Allā Jordan: their place and role in archaeological research,' *ADAJ* 43, 145-167.

Philip, G.
1989 *Metal Weapons of the Early and Middle Bronze Ages in Syria–Palestine* (BAR S 526/1.2), Oxford.

Pringle, D.
1984 'Thirteenth century pottery from the Monastery of St. Mary of Carmel,' *Levant* 16, 91-111.

Pringle, D.
1985 'Mediaeval Pottery from Caesarea: The Crusader Period,' *Levant* 17, 171-202.

Pritchard, J.B.
1980 *The Cemetery at Tell es-Sa'idiyeh, Jordan.* (University Museum Monograph 41), Philadelphia.

Pritchard, J.B.
1985 *Tell es-Sa^c^idiyeh. Excavations on the Tell, 1964-1966* (University Monograph 60), Philadelphia.

Rast, W.E.
1978 *Taanach I. Studies in the Iron Age Pottery,* Cambridge MA.

Redford D.B.
1992 *Egypt, Canaan and Israel in ancient Times,* Princeton New Yersey.

Reich, R.
2003 'Baking and Cooking at Masada,' *ZDPV* 119, 140-158.

Reicke, B. and L. Rost
1979 *Biblisch-Historisches Handwörterbuch IV. Register und Historisch-archäologische Karte Palästinas,* VandenHoeck & Rupprecht, Göttingen.

Riedl, N.
1999 'Eine neu entdeckte Meilensteingruppe in Nordwestjordanien,' *ZDPV* 115, 45-48.

Rowe, A.
1930 *The Topography and History of Beth-Shan,* Philadelphia.

Rowe, A.
1940 *The Four Canaanite Temples of Beth Shan 1,* Philadelphia.

Salje, B. *et al.* (eds)
2004 *Gesichter des Orients. 10 000 Jahre Kunst und Kultur aus Jordanien,* Mainz am Rhein.

Schumacher, G.
1890 *Northern 'Ajlūn, "within the Decapolis",* Watt, London.

Seger J.D. & H. Darell Lance,
1988 *Gezer V: The Field I Caves,* Hebrew Union College. Jerusalem.

Simons, J.
1937 *Handbook for the Study of the Egyptian Topographical Lists relating to Western Asia,* Leyden.

Sivan, D. & Z. Cochavi-Rainey
1992 *West Semitic Vocabulary in Egyptian Script of the 14th to the 10th Centuries BCE* (Studies by the Department of Bible and Ancient Near East VI), Beer-Sheva.

Smith, R.H.
1973 *Pella of the Decapolis. Vol.1 The 1967 Season of the College of Wooster Expedition to Pella,* Wooster.

Smith, R.H. and L.P. Day
1989 *Pella of the Decapolis. Vol. 2. Final Report on the College of Wooster Excavations in Area IX, The Civic Complex, 1979-1985,* Wooster.

Staubli, Th.
1991 *Das Image der Nomaden im Alten Israel und in der Ikonographie seiner sesshaften Nachbarn,* (OBO 107), Freiburg Schweiz, Göttingen.

Steel L. and C. McCarthy
2008 'Survey at Arediou Vouppes (Lithosouros), a Late Bronze Age agricultural settlement on Cyprus: a preliminary analysis of the material culture assemblages,' *BASOR* 351 (2008) 9-39.

Steen, E. van der
1991 'The Iron Age Bread Ovens from Tell Deir 'Alla,' *ADAJ* 35, 135-153.

Steen, E. van der
1996 'The Central East Jordan Valley in the Late Bronze and Early Iron Ages,' *BASOR* 302, 55-74.

Steuernagel, C.
1925 'Der ^c^Adschlun,' *ZDPV* 48, 1-144 (A.49-A.192).

Steuernagel, C.
1926 'Der ^c^Adschlun,' *ZDPV* 49, 1-167 (A.385-A.551).

Strange, J.
1997 'Tall al-Fukhār 1990-1991: A Preliminary Report,' *SHAJ* VI, 399-406.

Tubb, J.N.
1988 'Tell es-Sa'idiyeh: Preliminary Report on the First Three Seasons of Renewed Excavations,' *Levant* 20, 23-89.

Veenhof, K.R.
2001 *Geschichte des Alten Orients bis zur Zeit Alexanders des Großen,* (ATD Ergänzungsreihe Band 11), Göttingen.

Vieweger, D.
2002a 'The Tell Zera'a in the Wādī el-^c^Arab,' *Occident & Orient* 7/2, 12-14.

Vieweger, D.
2002b 'Tall Zar'a in the Wādī el-^c^Arab. The "Gadara-Region-Project",' *ADAJ* 46, 157-177.

Vieweger, D. and J. Häser
2005 'Der *Tell Zerā'a* im *Wādī el-^c^Arab*. Das 'Gadara Region Project' in den Jahren 2001-2004,' *ZDPV* 121, 1-30.

Vieweger, D. and J. Häser
2007a 'Das "Gadara Region Project". Der *Tell Zerā'a* in den Jahren 2005 und 2006,' *ZDPV* 123, 1-27.

Vieweger, D. and J. Häser
2007b 'Tall Zira'a. Five Thousand Years of Palestinian History on a Single-Settlement Mound,' *NEA* 70, 147-167.

Vilders, M.M.E.
1992a 'The Stratigraphy and the Pottery of Phase M at Deir 'Alla and the Date of the Plaster Texts,' *Levant* 24, 187-200.

Vilders, M.M. E
1992b 'Cooking Pots from Tell es-Sa^c^ideyeh,' *PEQ* 124, 162.

Vilders, M.M.E.
1993 'Some Remarks on the Production of Cooking Pots in the Jordan Valley,' *PEQ* 125, 149–156.

Vriezen, K.
2002a 'The Region of Gadara/Umm Qeis Project. Second Part of the 2001-Season. A Test Trench on Tell Zera'a,' *Occident & Orient* 7/1, 18-19.

Vriezen, K.
2002b 'Excavations at Tall Zar^ca,' *Munjazāt* 3, 9-10.

Vriezen, K.
2003 'The Region of Gadara/Umm Qeis Project. The 2002-Season. A Test Trench on Tell Zera'a,' *Occident & Orient* 8/1, 13-14.

Weber, T.M. and U. Hübner
1998 'Gadara 1998. The Excavation of the Five-aisled Basilica at Umm Qays: A Prelininary Report,' *ADAJ* 42, 443-455.

Weber, T.M.
2002 *Gadara - Umm Qēs I. Gadara Decapolitana. Untersuchungen zur Topographie, Geschichte, Architektur und der Bildenden Kunst einer "Polis Hellenis" im Ostjordanland (ADPV, 30)*, Wiesbaden .

Weiss, Z.
2005 *The Sepphoris Synagogue*, Jerusalem.

Wente, E.F.
1990 *Letters from Ancient Egypt*, (SBLWAW), Atlanta.

Werning, D.A.
2005 'Die Beth-Sche'an-Gedenkstele Sethos' I.,' in: B. Janowski & G.Wilhelm (eds), *Texte aus der Umwelt des Alten Testaments. Neue Folge Band 2*, Gütersloh.

Wilkinson, A.
1971 *Ancient Egyptian Jewellery*, London.

Worschech, U.
1992 '*Collared-Rim Jars* aus Moab Anmerkungen zur Entwicklung und Verbreitung der Krüge mit „Halswulst",' *ZDPV* 108, 149–153.

Yadin, Y.
1962 *James A. de Rothshield expedition at Hazor. II. An account of the second season of excavations, 1956*, Jerusalem.

Yadin, Y.
1963 *The art of warfare in biblical lands in the light of archaeological discovery*, London.

Yaholam-Mack, N.
2007 'Groundstone Tools and Objects,' in: A.Mazar and R.A. Mullins (eds), *Excavations at Tel Beth-Shean 1989-1996 Volume II. The Middle and Late Bronze Age Strata in Area R*, The Israel Exploration Society, Jerusalem, 639-660.

Yon, M.
1981 *Dictionnaire illustré multilingue de la céramique du Proche Orient Ancien* (Collection de la maison de l'orient méditerranéen Bo 10, Série archéologique, 7) Lyon-Paris.

Yoyotte, J.
1999 'La stèle de Ramsès II à Keswé et sa signification historique*,' *BSFE* 140, 44–58.

Yurco, J.J.
1986 'Merenptah's Canaanite Campaign,' *JARCE* 23, 189–215.

Ziadeh, G.
1995 'Ottoman Ceramics from Ti'innik, Palestine,' *Levant* 27, 209-245.

Zwickel, W.
1994 *Der Tempelkult in Kanaan und Israel* (Forschungen zum Alten Testament 10), Tübingen.

www.ingramcontent.com/pod-product-compliance
Lightning Source LLC
Chambersburg PA
CBHW051307270326
41926CB00030B/4751